DAMAGED DISCIPLES

Casualties of
Authoritarian Churches and
the Shepherding Movement

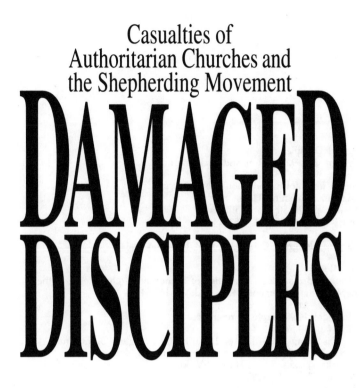

DAMAGED DISCIPLES

RON & VICKI BURKS

ZondervanPublishingHouse
Academic and Professional Books
Grand Rapids, Michigan

A Division of HarperCollins*Publishers*

Damaged Disciples
Copyright © 1992 by Ron and Vicki Burks

Requests for information should be addressed to:
Zondervan Publishing House
Academic and Professional Books
Grand Rapids, Michigan 49530

Library of Congress Cataloging-in-Publication Data

Burks, Ron.
    Damaged disciples : casualties of authoritarian churches and the
shepherding movement / Ron and Vicki Burks.
        p.   cm.
    Includes bibliographical references.
    ISBN 0-310-57611-3
    1. Discipling (Christianity) 2. Authority (Religion) 3. Control
(Psychology)–Religious aspects–Christianity. 4. Burks, Ron.
5. Burks, Vicki.   I. Burks, Vicki.   II. Title.
BV4520.B87   1992
262'.8–dc20   91-44732
                                                                        CIP

Edited by Jan M. Ortiz
Cover design by Jack Foster
Cover illustration by Corey Wilkinson

Printed in the United States of America

92 93 94 95 96 / AM / 10 9 8 7 6 5 4 3 2 1

*To everyone to whom the words of a pastor
have become wounds to the soul*

CONTENTS

FOREWORD

In recent years I have counseled with several troubled Christians who have needed to talk about a rather unusual problem. They all expressed appreciation for the churches they had once attended—the worship services, the preaching, and how helpful the people had been to one another. But in each instance there seemed to be an underlying anger that was affecting their present growth in grace. Though expressed differently, the common denominator was that they were all former members of churches that practiced a very authoritative form of church government. They had been influenced in one way or another by the Discipleship/Shepherding Movement. Since leaving those churches they seemed unable to form new Christian relationships. Sometimes they had trouble with any genuine friendships, and found it difficult, often almost impossible, to feel comfortable in other church surroundings. Worst of all, they were unable to trust others—sometimes this even included the Lord himself. They now seemed confused and ambivalent about their faith.

Most of them agreed that many of their experiences and relationships had been helpful at the time. Some of the scriptural insights were meaningful but many of the doctrines and practices had been damaging. They needed help in sorting the true from the false if they were to recover a growing relationship with God. Church growth and Christian discipleship are prominent and important topics today. There are several varieties representing some of the mainstreams of the church that contain a solid theological basis. The popular and extremely helpful *Master Plan* books by Robert Coleman, the church-growth principles set forth by the Arns, and Allan Coppedge's *Biblical Principles of Discipleship* are bearing fruit worldwide. But many have been so confused by the discipleship/shepherding extremes they miss the truths of those more properly balanced. Because people were attracted to the movement from many mainline denominations, they did not have much knowledge of Scripture and often lacked solid theological roots. They now find themselves disillusioned and fearful. They sometimes present unique problems to leaders from whom they seek counseling. Both pastors and congregations need to know how to minister to their special needs and how to accomplish the difficult task of integrating them into their congregations.

Professional counselors are often at a loss when dealing with such persons. One of my colleagues reported that in her practice she found them hurt and wary of any kind of the deep fellowship that characterizes true body life in the church. I have seen serious psychological damage caused by these movements. Often it reaches a peak when former members reach mid-life, and pre-existing, unresolved personality problems come to the surface. The repressive relationships and the pattern of giving up personal autonomy to a pastor/leader can result in a loss of identity and self-confidence. These factors combined with poor theology often lead people to a sense of betrayal, to being "trapped," and to general depression.

This book will assist pastoral and professional counselors who are trying to help such people out of their confusion. The methods described in the final chapter were developed and are now being used in Ron and Vicki's extensive counseling ministry to former members.

Ron and Vicki write not as outside observers but as those who actually experienced what they describe. Actually, they are on their own personal journey back to the Cross—the only source of our wholeness. Thus they are able to engagingly relate their own story in a way that seems to engender trust in the reader so that the Holy Spirit can bring healing to such counselees. This is a book written from the inside. My hope is that it will enable many to find light and freedom from that which, for them, was a kind of "dark night of the soul."

David Seamands

ACKNOWLEDGMENTS

Without Philip and Michele Spottswood, we would still be saying, "After what we've been through, we should write a book." They invested both time and money to make sure this book was written.

Dr. David Seamands took time from his incredibly busy schedule to read the entire manuscript and graciously agreed to write the Foreword. His encouragement was welcome during the long approval process.

Other members of the faculty of Asbury Theological Seminary, helped solidify the ideas in the last four chapters. Dr. David Bauer, professor of English Bible, graciously corrected my occasional bits of "imprecise thinking," and his considerable expertise adds extra weight to statements we made like, "The New Testament does not teach. . . ." Any remaining "imprecise thinking" is not in the chapters he examined. Dr. Fred Layman, professor of Biblical Theology, reviewed various sections and we made extensive use of his insights. Dr. Harold Burgess encouraged us in the project, saw promise in our efforts, and contributed greatly to getting this book published.

Velma Buzbee, Vicki's mother, knowing full well how we, and our four active children, would completely alter her lifestyle still opened her home to us for the entire summer while we wrote.

Our children, David, Amanda, Ami, and Megan saw

only the back of Vicki's or my head silhouetted against the green glow of the computer screen for three months.

To my father, whose dedication and support made this project even thinkable.

My mother, a former schoolteacher, spent a summer tutoring me because she felt my elementary school was not properly emphasizing traditional phonics. She made sure I could read and write, but never knew of this fruit of her labor. She died May 12, 1991 from the effects of Alzheimer's disease.

And finally, to Jerry and Tisha Moore and Mark and Teresa Alexander who helped us trust again.

INTRODUCTION

Popular writers define discipleship as some sort of individualized or small-group training of new converts. Books abound that teach one form of discipleship or another. Discipleship or disciple making, is taught by many to be the biblical way to make new converts into mature Christians, and eventually into disciple-makers themselves. A stirring testimony of effective evangelistic outreach or dramatic church growth is usually included in these books.

But there is another definition of discipleship, often labeled "shepherding," that has come to be defined as a form of committed relationship between an experienced Christian and a new, or otherwise inexperienced, believer. In this relationship, some of the disciple-maker's Christian maturity is imparted to the disciple because of the disciple's obedience to the disciple-maker's authority. Intense, small-group and one-on-one teaching and experiences bring the disciple into a position of spiritual maturity. The shepherding relationship, which we simply called "Discipleship," is intended to be permanent, to extend into all areas of the disciple's life, and to become the foundation of church structure. *Christianity Today* attached the name shepherding movement[1] to this type of church and Christian organizational structure. Today there are many churches and several major Christian organizations whose structure fits the *Christianity Today* label. The shepherding movement that we discuss in this book began in Fort Lauderdale, Florida and is centered today in Mobile, Alabama. The original leaders of this movement were Bob Mumford, Derek Prince, Don Basham, and Charles Simpson, and the basic principles they taught influenced countless individuals and many other movements and groups.

At its peak, the shepherding movement directly involved fewer than 50,000 people and indirectly involved another 50,000.[2] However, a far larger number of people were affected. *New Wine Magazine*, the main forum for shepherding teaching, with almost 90,000 subscriptions at its peak circulation, was much larger, at that time, than was *Christianity Today*. It went into over 120 countries. In addition, from 1970 to 1985 as many as 500,000 audio tapes a year were mailed from Fort Lauderdale and Mobile that shared the vision, goals, and teaching of the shepherding movement.

At one time there were shepherding-related churches of various sizes in most major cities in the English-speaking world. Countless other independent and denominational churches were influenced by the teaching of the movement. At least two other networks of churches patterned their organizational structure according to the movement's teaching.

Many readers and listeners used these concepts in their own churches and prayer meetings. Leaders within the Roman Catholic Church saw similarities to their tradition in the movement's doctrines and formed "shepherding" communities within their church.

Literally thousands of independent disciple-makers gathered like groups around themselves. Some of these inflicted very malignant forms of abuse on their followers, according to Christian and secular counselors. One example, the "Crossroads" movement, is described in great detail in Flavil R. Yeakley's book, *The Discipleship Dilemma*.

Other disciple-makers have reached, independently, more or less the same conclusions as the four teachers listed above. Dr. Keith Phillips reaches very similar conclusions in his book, *The Making of a Disciple*.

Many of the ideas of the shepherding movement were quite controversial twenty years ago. Some, such as the understanding of submission of wives to husbands, seem to have taken their place in the mainstream of current evangelical thought. Although many people apparently have been, and continue to be, helped by the teaching and practice of this form of discipleship, it has also damaged tens of thousands of lives. Jack Hayford has said of the shepherding movement,

> Multiplied hundreds of pastors, like myself, have spent large amounts of time over the last 15 years picking up the pieces of broken lives that resulted from distortion of truth by extreme teachings and destructive applications on discipleship, authority, and shepherding.[3]

Members of the Maranatha Christian Churches, a group greatly influenced by the shepherding movement, have encountered similar problems.

> Many former members have reported fearing that leaving the group was tantamount to leaving God's will and that this could result in retribution of some kind: a heart attack or car accident—even the loss of salvation.[4]

Dr. Flavil Yeakley, a sociologist and church-growth consultant, studied another shepherding-type group associated with the Churches of Christ that was strongly influenced by the teaching of the shepherding movement. He instructs ministers and counselors working with former members of that group that:

> You need to be able to reach and restore the many dropouts who will be harmed psychologically and spiritually by their participation in this movement. The time when these problems are most likely to develop is when the young

people in this movement reach mid-life. Falsification of psychological type (trying to change your personality to imitate that of another) produces a serious mid-life crisis. There will be major burn-out problems, serious depression, and a variety of other psychological and spiritual problems to resolve.[4]

Later in his book, while explaining the size of the problem, he reports:

Counselors in virtually every city where this radical movement exists are now being virtually flooded with clients who are the psychological, emotional, and spiritual victims of this authoritarian movement. Psychologists, who specialize in treating cult victims have reported that in several cities they are now treating more people from these discipling congregations than from all other groups put together.[5]

There is some debate as to whether these groups that stress authoritarian discipleship should be called cults. Yeakley does not find the term "cult" very meaningful, and we agree with him. "Cult" is laden with too much emotion and not enough clarity—it evokes response without revealing content.

Those who do regard these movements as cults often cite the charismatic leader of the People's Temple, Jim Jones, and the resulting Jonestown, Guyana tragedy, as an example of the abuse of Christian authority. While preparing this book we have listened to the testimony of and have spoken personally with Bonnie Thielmann, Jim Jones's "adopted" daughter, and former member of his People's Temple. Bonnie told us that frequently in his public meetings Jim Jones would hold up a Bible, express his contempt for it, throw it on the floor, and spit on it. He would then dare God, if he existed, to strike him dead. When nothing happened, he pretended to display supernatural gifts of knowledge and healing, which he declared were his alone. Then, when Bonnie left the People's Temple, she was attacked, beaten, and raped by individuals identifying themselves as Jim Jones's enforcers. Nothing remotely like this ever happened in the shepherding movement. Thus, comparisons some so glibly made between shepherding/discipling groups and the People's Temple showed a profound ignorance of both movements and a callous attitude toward fellow Christians. These comparisons only served to deepen confusion and misunderstanding.

But, what about the concerns expressed by Jack Hayford and others? There *are* serious problems associated with shepherding churches. Former followers often feel bruised and burned out. They feel alienated from other believers and from God. We have seen leaders in shepherding churches, either consciously or unconsciously, use subtle verbal and psychological manipulation to exercise control over their followers. Some of this manipulation has been recognized and stopped, according to shepherding leaders. However, we believe the problems with the movement are much more serious than a few isolated instances of abuse of authority.

In recent years, many of the leaders of the shepherding movement have apologized or repented for things done and said in the name of discipleship. The leaders, it seems, are the only ones who have ever had a story to tell or a confession to make. This book is different. It is written for, about, and by, those we call followers.

Most followers in the shepherding movement knew the founders and leaders only through their tapes and magazine articles. We were followers of the teachers individually, before they came together, and before there was a shepherding movement. We had the opportunity to meet and know them personally for a time and followed them for almost twenty years. Vicki and I are perhaps unique in that while we were close in some ways to the leaders we were always followers. We never led a care group; we never pastored. We followed the leaders of the movement from 1969 until 1988.

I say we, because this book contains the experiences of the two of us, both husband and wife, each particularly called and gifted, accepted and beloved by God through Jesus Christ, though it did not always seem that way. . . .

All teachings related in this book are from our own notes and recollections, or from the public record. Most of the applications of the teaching are ours alone, or those with whom we have directly shared these experiences. The experiences of others are included, but what they said, without documentation about the teaching or actions of third parties is not. Hearsay has been avoided.

We have conducted interviews with other followers of shepherding churches in preparation for this book. These interviews have shown us that our experiences are shared by a large and growing number of Christians.

Our reasons for writing this book are not to confront, expose, lay blame, hurt, or vindicate. Rather, we have four purposes: (1) To examine specific practices and teachings of the shepherding movement. (2) To provide a resource for you to be able to meaningfully evaluate the form of Christian discipleship you are involved in. (3) To provide a means of healing for those who have been injured by this, and other similar forms of shepherding-discipleship. (4) To provide a resource for those who minister to those hurt by this and other similar movements.

In 2 Samuel 24:15, we find that within the kingdom of God it is often the people who suffer most when leaders make mistakes.

> So the Lord sent a plague on Israel from that morning until the end of the time designated, and seventy thousand of the people from Dan to Beersheba died.

The context of this Scripture reveals the great suffering of King David, his repentance for his sin, and even his wish that the punishment would be only upon him. But punishment for David alone was not to be. Instead seventy thousand people died and seventy thousand families were decimated because the king had made a mistake! "Why do we suffer for his rebellion?", a bitter, lonely wife and mother might have cried, "How can he still go on and be king?" We can relate.

It is because God cares greatly for those who pay the price for a leader's mistake, that this book has been written.

1

THE WORDS OF LIFE

THE FORMAL APOLOGIES

The use and abuse of authority is at the center of the controversy surrounding the shepherding movement. Authority and the effect it had on interpersonal relationships distinguished the movement from every other church and Christian organization.

The shepherding movement began in a motel room in Fort Lauderdale, Florida, in the fall of 1970. Ever since that time the leaders seem to have been apologizing for it. Public apologies for abuses of authority by those in middle and lower levels of leadership have appeared in print, on CBN, and at conferences. The most recent apology was in November, 1989 at the Ridgecrest, North Carolina, conference of Christian Believers United. On the second night of the conference, Bob Mumford, one of the founders, read a statement of apology for his involvement in the movement. In it he blamed the abuses of the movement on mistakes in orthopraxis, the specific applications or practices of the movement, rather than orthodoxy, or the doctrines of the movement. In effect, he was saying that what the four teachers had taught was right, but the applications of those teachings were flawed.

Derek Prince, the key-note speaker for the evening, made a similar, albeit, impromptu statement expressing his conviction that though he felt God had drawn the four leaders together he had never intended to start a movement.

TEACHERS BECOME LEADERS

In the fall of 1970, four traveling Bible teachers who had frequently ministered together, but did not really know each other personally, met for prayer. Their gathering was in response to the recent revelation of the gross immorality of a Christian leader and mutual friend. As they prayed and talked, they came to the realization that their constant travel isolated them from their families and from any form of church oversight. They felt that they too were vulnerable to temptation. Then and there they made a covenant to be accountable to each other. The specific implications of this decision were not immediately obvious to them, but all have testified that something deeply spiritual occurred at that meeting.

They were ahead of their time. The idea of avoiding temptation through mutual accountability was a radical shift for the Charismatic movement, which stressed the believer's "freedom in the Spirit." (Revelations of the moral and ethical conduct of other Christian leaders in recent years are testimony of their sensitivity to God.) The news of their "covenant" was met with a fire storm of controversy. They were accused of trying to turn the freewheeling charismatic movement into another denomination, which through the accusations, the ridicule, and the open contempt that followed only served to cement their relationships to each other.

Ironically, none was a churchman much interested in denominational politics, committees, or polity. Initially, they were Bible teachers who just wanted closer fellowship with one another. But many young pastors, and in my own case, would-be pastors, were drawn to their teaching on discipleship and the church. We could sense the spiritual security they talked so much about. We wanted the same protection from temptation and the same encouragement in righteousness that their relationships seemed to give them. We also recognized the anointing to minister that they had and desired it for ourselves.

The following are not formal biographies; rather they are what we knew and believed about these remarkable men.

Derek Prince

Derek Prince was by far the most experienced of the group. His British manner and decorum enabled him to minister in the miraculous power of God without a hint of manipulative emotionalism.

His primary emphasis was on what he felt were the essentials of Christianity, the work of the Cross, the new birth, water baptism, and the gifts of the Spirit. Like the others, he did not believe that the gifts of the Spirit, listed in 1 Corinthians 12, were optional, but standard equipment for all believers. They were God's empowerment available to believers both for meeting the needs in their own walks with God and enabling them to minister effectively to the needs of others. The burden of Prince's heart was always for the believer's foundation in the Scriptures. To this end, he wrote over twenty-five books, the latest of which is *Blessing or Curse, You Can Choose*. He wrote and personally produced and distributed numerous Bible study correspondence courses, follow-up materials, and systematic Bible expositions to supplement his extensive public speaking and radio ministry. The importance of committed, disciplined fellowship in the church was a major theme of his teaching.

Born in India, he was educated at Eton College and Cambridge University. He was a professor of philosophy at Kings College, Cambridge. A Greek scholar prior to becoming a Christian, Derek Prince learned Hebrew and Aramaic at Hebrew University in Jerusalem. We understood that his personal Scripture devotions were often in the original languages. In spite of his formidable educational credentials, he was not interested in writing formal commentaries, a formal systematic theology, or other scholarly pursuits typical of a theologian. He was, and is, a popularizer, ministering the Word of God to multitudes wherever he goes.

He was a minister in Palestine during the birth of the nation of Israel where he met his first wife, Lydia. Several years older than Derek, she was a missionary caring for eight young girls who had been orphaned in the conflict. Some were Jewish and some were Arab. They adopted them all. Much of his ministry has centered around his love for Israel and Jerusalem. Their last daughter was adopted during their time as missionaries to Kenya.

At a New Wine conference in Fort Lauderdale in 1972, I introduced my wife of a few weeks, Vicki, to Derek and Lydia. Lydia, took one look at her and asked, "Are you in total subjection to your husband?" displaying her apparent disdain for the popular teaching. Vicki, blushing, replied, "I–I–I think so." Derek facetiously remarked, "But only when it suits you, eh?" He smiled kindly and they walked away.

After Lydia's death, he married his second wife, Ruth, and they now divide their meager time off the road between homes in Israel and Fort Lauderdale. For reasons never made entirely clear to us in the movement, he dissolved his formal ties to the others around 1984.

Don Basham

Gentle and plain spoken, Don Basham's laid-back, sensible, and humorous presentation of the spiritual gifts made him a leader in the rapidly expanding charismatic movement in the late sixties and early seventies. A former Disciples of Christ minister, his messages and ten popular books like *Face Up With A Miracle*, *Lead Us Not Into Temptation*, *Handbook on Holy Spirit Baptism*, and *Deliver Us From Evil* are filled with personal warmth, humor, and clear instructions for Christians at all levels of spiritual maturity.

He was not only a pastor, but also a dedicated family man. He is known for his sense of humor and used countless humorous personal stories in his books and sermons that always reflected his high esteem for his wife Alice, their five children, and many grandchildren. For me, his was an example of what biblical family life should be like. His sense of humor never seemed to suffer in the face of his heavy schedule. One Sunday, after an exhausting meeting at a conference, ten or twelve of us, who were lunching together, were making our way back from the salad bar one by one, absent-mindedly beginning our meal. Suddenly we all remembered we had not said the blessing. We all looked at Don and he looked up and said piously, "Bless this food O my Lord, and all that is within me!"

The Way I See It tells his story using the short episodes originally printed in his column by the same name in *New Wine Magazine*, which he edited after the shepherding movement became established. He pastored churches in Washington, D.C. and Canada before making his decision to leave the salaried ministry to "walk by faith." His decision became one of our principle "doctrines" for ministry.

Don Basham never wanted to be controversial. His

demeanor was more suited to his interests as a hunter, fisherman, and private pilot. His fatherly appearance was not that of a controversial man. But ministry opportunities brought him time and again to the Scriptures and the ministry of Jesus. His books, public ministry of healing, teaching on the gifts of the Spirit, and deliverance from evil spirits (which he testified to learning from Derek Prince) attracted controversy from both Pentecostals and mainline denominations alike. His *The Most Dangerous Game* on the occult, set many on the path to freedom. Again and again we heard stories about how his fearless attention to uncomfortable or unpopular issues made him a target of someone's disdain.

His sense of humor made the rejection and controversy bearable. Over lunch one day in 1971 Don remarked that, while the fried chicken we were eating was good, he would rather have been eating Chinese food. Alice frowned at him and said, "Honestly Don, I think you have a spirit of Chinese food!" Don replied playfully in a squeaky other-worldly voice, "That's not a spirit! There's no such thing as a Chinese-food spirit!"

Don Basham, a loveable man who had one of the most powerful deliverance ministries of his day, managed, back then, to avoid taking himself too seriously. He went to be with the Lord in 1988.

Bob Mumford

Bob Mumford was the best known of all the Bible teachers who met that day in the Fort Lauderdale motel room. Bob Mumford served four years in the Navy, the source of many of his hilarious stories, after a dramatic experience with God brought him back to his Pentecostal roots. He received his M.Div. from Reformed Episcopal Seminary in Philadelphia. Once Billy Graham's favorite Bible teacher, he served as a pastor and was dean of men and professor of Bible and missions for a time at Elim Bible Institute in Lima, New York. He and Judy raised four children while part of the shepherding movement.

He was also the first to influence me about the importance of discipleship. His ability to combine raucous humor and complex spiritual truth was unparalleled. He once told me that he had carefully studied the humor style and timing of Bill Cosby. It was once said about him that "he gets your lips out of the way with a laugh so he can hit you in the mouth with the truth without drawing blood." So vocal were his audiences that, after making a profound point, when there was no response, he often asked, "Are you breathing?"

He liked to say that his emphasis was on the how-tos of Christianity. The truth is, his practical teaching on the Scriptures went far beyond that. His series of taped messages, *The Spirit of Truth and Error*, delivered at Melodyland Christian Center long before his involvement with the shepherding movement remains for me one of the most profound treatments of basic theology that I have ever encountered. His principle of "truth held in tension" helped explain the many paradoxes of the Christian faith.

His insightful and humorous description of the trials in the Christian life in his book, *The Purpose and Principle of Temptation*, were an encouraging balance to the doctrine of name-it-and-claim-it faith then prevalent in the charismatic movement. During his years in the movement his ministry centered around what can be called the "now" word to the church, that is, what might the Lord be saying today about the nature, purpose, and structure of the church. His ministry was prophetic in that it challenged the charismatic movement to focus more on learning God's ways than on seeking his power.

He has authored many articles and books, among them, *Christ in Session, Living Happily Ever After, The*

Problem of Doing Your Own Thing and *The King and You*. He continues to publish his newsletter, *Plumbline*. He withdrew from the movement in 1986, after moving from Mobile to northern California.

Charles Simpson

Charles Simpson is the least known, but the most influential inside the shepherding movement, of all the teachers. He attended New Orleans Theological Seminary while pastoring the three-hundred-member Bayview Heights Baptist Church in Mobile, Alabama. During a time of personal spiritual drought, a friend gave him a biography of Charles G. Finney. Through Finney's testimony of receiving a "mighty baptism with the Holy Spirit," and the experience of a friend Charles Simpson was swept into the early Charismatic revival. He became a favorite speaker at Full Gospel Business Men's Meetings.

As a Southern Baptist pastor involved in the Charismatic revival, the condition of the denominational churches concerned him. One Saturday night I picked him up at Dulles airport and by the time we had arrived at the hotel it was after midnight. His connections had been such that he had not eaten since morning. The restaurant was closed, but the bellman assured us we could order a sandwich in the Garden Room. Eager to serve the man of God, I said, "Great," and we were led to a table. After we ordered, the lights came up and we discovered we were at one of the front tables in the hotel lounge. The singer was returning from his break and began to lead the suddenly very animated crowd in a popular song. Arms around shoulders, they sang loudly and swayed to the rhythm. Charles Simpson leaned over the table and shouted, which was the only way he could be heard, "I think there is more fellowshiping going on in here right now than there will be tomorrow in most churches."

He was the first to "receive disciples." While he was still a Baptist pastor, his church's former parsonage was used as housing for disciple interns. In 1972 he moved to Fort Lauderdale where he continued to receive disciples. Later, he returned to the Gulf Coast and became the only one of the original four to actually build a local church based on discipling relationships.

Although he has been acknowledged as a pastor, disciple-maker, and administrator, his primary gift is as a teacher and public speaker. Beneath his down-home humor and southern accent is a remarkable gift for storytelling which, when applied to expositing Bible passages, often transports the listener into the story.

As did Mumford's, Simpson's interests centered on the now word for the church. His emphasis differed from Bob Mumford's in that his ministry was directed more to the followers' relationships to each other and to their leaders.

His teachings in 1971 on discipleship, fellowship, and worship became the cornerstones of the shepherding movement. His approach, sometimes attributed by others to Juan Carlos Ortiz,[1] connected disciple-making and church government in a radical way. This one issue is the distinctive characteristic of his teaching that affected so many lives, churches, and movements.

He was subsequently given organizational authority and exercised considerable influence in the movement and apparently over the other teachers. He alone remains at the head of a defacto denomination of discipling churches called the Fellowship of Covenant Ministers and Churches.

Ern Baxter

W. Ern Baxter was not present in that Florida hotel room. His association with the others came much later.

He seemed to fill the intellectual void when Derek Prince left. One of the first things one noticed about the ministry of Ern Baxter was his astonishing command of the English language and it came as a surprise to learn that he held no advanced degrees. His enormous vocabulary and impeccable grammar made him unquestionably the most skilled orator of the group.

His gift for storytelling, or his "sanctified imagination," as we called it, allowed him to harmonize the gospel and prophetic accounts of the life of Jesus in entertaining ways. His story from Matthew 27:53 of Jesus pre-resurrection visit to the gates of the prison of the righteous dead and his demand of Satan for the keys was not the meat of his teaching, but it was certainly the spice. In the storytelling, verses establishing Jesus authority over Satan became lines of dialogue. Jesus "binds the strongman," takes his keys and "plunders his house" of the saints he has held prisoner in death.

Over fifty years in the ministry have seen him ministering all over the world. In the late forties and early fifties, during his association with the late evangelist, William Branam, he ministered to crowds numbering more than 80,000.

Except for Derek Prince's, Baxter's ministry was the only one that centered on the person and work of Christ. His messages, grounded in Reformed theology, on the place of the believer in Christ were the only messages (in our memories) where we heard in detail the totality of Christ's finished work on the Cross.

He brought a much needed biblical and intellectual foundation to the highly experience-oriented charismatic movement. As far as we know, he has not made a public statement with regard to his current involvement in the movement.

LARGER THAN LIFE

The leaders of the shepherding movement were seemingly larger than life. All were excellent communicators and gifted Bible teachers. Their messages or teachings typically lasted over an hour and a half per session, yet each could hold audiences of thousands enthralled. They were always entertaining but never cute.

By the time of their involvement in the shepherding movement they had all traveled around the world and were household names in the charismatic movement. They were a diverse group, British, Canadian, southern, northern, and midwestern; they were scholarly, intense, humorous, laid back, practical, and idealistic.

Derek Prince, who grew up as an Anglican but was led to salvation by Pentecostals, blamed the Anglican Church for never teaching him about salvation. Later he was publicly attacked by his fellow Pentecostals for his belief that a Christian could "have" demons. The Southern Baptists repeatedly tried to vote Charles Simpson out. Bob Mumford grew up Pentecostal, but his pre-shepherding association with Derek Prince and other charismatics rankled Pentecostals.

Thus, their ecclesiology was inclusive. They believed the true church crossed all denominational lines to include all who follow Christ in any given locality. They left no room for a view of the church as an institution separate from daily life. All traveled widely and were "world Christians." They all saw the church as a worldwide body of believers

As a result, most were expelled or "encouraged" to leave their denominations because of their loyalty to God and to what they found in the Scriptures. Later, they were even rejected by their peers because of their commitment to each other. They had all paid a dear price for their call to the ministry. Michael Harper commended their restraint in handling the frequent criticism.[2] With leaders like these, we could do no less than follow, and expect no more from other Christians than they had received.

Their apparent total commitment to one another was the basis for our commitments to each other, and ultimately, to one of them. How could a movement founded by these strong and dedicated men become so destructive to the spiritual lives of so many? Why didn't their accountability to each other and their willingness to apologize to critics prevent the abuses and damage to our lives?

2

WHAT BEGAN IN THE SPIRIT

You need to be able to reach and restore the many drop-outs who will be harmed psychologically and spiritually by their participation in this movement. The time when these problems are most likely to develop is when the young people in this movement reach mid-life. Falsification of psychological type (trying to change your personality to imitate that of another) produces a serious mid-life crisis. There will be major burn-out problems, serious depression, and a variety of other psychological and spiritual problems to resolve.[1]

Yeakley's comment is of particular interest to Vicki and me because we came into the shepherding movement as young people. During recent years as we face mid-life, we, and many of our friends, are experiencing the very same symptoms Yeakley predicts for young people now involved in the movement he studied.

This book is about how we have been able to find the grace to go on and serve God. There is a way. The price has been high, too high for some of our friends who face broken lives and broken marriages. Sadly, the price we paid was not the one required in the Scriptures to follow Jesus.

To understand where we are, it may help to know

something about us and how we became a part of the shepherding movement. Our stories are not unique. There was no deep void in our souls that cried out for domination. For most of us it just wasn't that simple.

RON

My father never worked for the famous computer company, but growing up in the fifties, I learned at a very young age, the real meaning behind the letters IBM—I've Been Moved. As an engineering program manager for a major aerospace contractor and eventually for NASA, my father worked on every manned space effort from the X-15 and Mercury capsules in the fifties and early sixties to the Space Shuttle.

My mother was a professional housewife. She packed and unpacked our lives with warmth and ease. I learned at a young age not to fear change. Wherever we lived, her work outside the home was for various garden clubs and civic organizations. She always managed to fit into the society of any city in which we lived.

Our frequent moves always seemed to be in and out of Huntsville, Alabama. Outside of Huntsville, we always joined the closest friendly church. At different times we were Methodist or Presbyterian, but in Huntsville, we always belonged to First Christian Church. For my parents, church was never associated with a rigid, detailed belief system. It was just the place where friendly people got together and did nice things. Doctrines and labels had no meaning for me. As an only child, my friends at church were more like family. I don't remember having to be made to go to church. It just seemed like the natural thing to do on Sunday.

Because of the church, I began Huntsville High School with a set of "lifelong" friends, even though I had not actually grown up with them. The church was always near the center of my family and social life. That is what I thought church should be.

After leaving for Florida State University in 1967, I attended the Christian Church in Tallahassee. It was a good church, but it was not home, and I wanted more. One evening, I went to a sorority house to visit a girl I had met on campus. She was not in, but there was a large, loud meeting going on in the parlor. A well-known football star was telling the sordid tale of his life without Christ and the difference a "personal relationship" with Christ had made. I sat in the back, fascinated. At the end of the meeting, they announced the formation of several small groups, which seemed to me to be the way to get to know these interesting people. Within a week, I found myself in a Campus Crusade for Christ Action Group, learning, by role-playing, how to share the Four Spiritual Laws. When I saw the diagrams in the little book, I realized that Christ did not have the preeminent place in my life that I wanted him to have. As we prayed the printed prayer in the training session, I really meant it.

Walking home that night, God, the Bible, the Cross, and all I had learned in church seemed to make sense. It was not a great emotional experience but I knew something had happened. Christ had come into my life in an entirely new way and it all fit into the context of a small, committed group. In the following months, I experienced the power and encouragement of that small group. It felt right. It felt like family. I had found what I had been looking for.

I spent the summer of 1968 on the kitchen staff at the Campus Crusade for Christ headquarters at Arrowhead Springs, California. My work schedule permitted me to audit Institute of Biblical Studies training courses. Hal Lindsey taught New Testament Survey. Bible Study Methods was taught by Harold Lindsell, editor of the Harper Study Bible. Tim LaHaye taught a course in

Christian life. I soon became accustomed to the most exciting Bible teaching evangelicalism had to offer.

As the sixties drew to a close, university campuses were the focal point of great changes in American society. Florida State was no exception. Bomb threats, sit-ins, demonstrations, and open-microphone free-speech rallies generally made those great years to be in college. In this atmosphere of radicalism it seemed appropriate to me that Christianity should be a radical commitment to the cause of Christ. I felt that we Christians should be just as committed as were the Weathermen or the Students for a Democratic Society. They were willing to go to jail for what they believed. I had also learned that Lenin had committed himself to be a lifelong revolutionary to the cause of the proletariat. I remember making a similar resolution regarding the cause of Christ.

Along with four other Christian men, I lived in a house that became a focal point of Campus Crusade activity. Bob Sutton, one of my house mates, was the leader of the large Crusade meetings. Another, Gerrit Gustafson, was involved in InterVarsity and was a Methodist student pastor. Tom and Dave, the other two, combined their deep love for God with hilarious good humor. I learned to love my "new brothers" and found, in combination with their fellowship, the grace of God to withstand the many temptations of college life.

We had frequent prayer meetings. During them we sometimes prayed for the high-school girls who were members of a small group that Dave was leading in the nearby town of Monticello. Unbeknown to me at the time, one of the girls, Vicki Buzbee, would become very special.

At "His Place," as our men's house was called that 1968–69 school year, our evening meal was always special. It began with a reading from Oswald Chambers' classic, *My Utmost for His Highest*, followed by prayer. As we proceeded through the readings day by day, all of us had to admit that we had not committed our utmost, and were not walking in his highest. We felt that there must be more to the Christian life and that that "something more" had to do with knowing Jesus better and loving each other more as Christians. Several experiences brought us to new understandings in both areas.

Bob Sutton had also been at Arrowhead in the summer of 1968, but had driven the twenty miles further into the mountains to Blue Jay for a few nights to hear Jon Braun, a former Campus Crusade speaker. What Bob heard changed his whole attitude about church.

Braun's idea of the noninstitutional church was that church could be an informal meeting in a home, complete with sacraments, baptisms, weddings, and everything else connected with regular churches. The concept fit comfortably with the upbringing I had had in the Christian church. I began to read some of the writings of Watchman Nee, and Nee's emphasis on the doctrine of the city church seemed biblical to me. As I saw it, there was one true church in every city, made up of the Christians within each organized church. This meant that small groups of the type we had experienced as part of Campus Crusade could actually be a church. The local Crusade staff, however, did not agree.

I returned to Arrowhead Springs for the summer of 1969 full of new ideas and experiences. After the Institute of Biblical Studies wrapped up its month of classes, I visited Jack Sparks, and his newly formed Christian World Liberation Front at the University of California, Berkeley. At the time, Berkeley was notorious for its radicalism, demonstrations, and atmosphere of political unrest. Sparks emphasis on Christianity as a radical subculture confirmed my own feelings of radicalism and challenged me to a lifestyle of resisting the status quo, in Jesus' name. I almost transferred to Berkeley, to join his movement.

That fall, Derek Prince arrived in Tallahassee and, in a series of meetings, he presented the church as being a place where believers and unbelievers alike could go to have their needs met through the power of God. A church that ministered like Jesus ministered was vastly different from the ones I knew, with their buses, carpets, and whites-only membership. During Prince's meetings I experienced a new dimension of the Holy Spirit. We called it "the Baptism of the Holy Spirit."

Campus Crusade for Christ eventually was not able to accept my experience or that of my friends. The lead staff member very reluctantly asked us to stop attending meetings. We accepted what we dubbed the "left foot of fellowship" and began to apply what we had learned about the church toward forming our own fellowship. Bob Sutton and others organized a charismatic conference at the Catholic student center—the only campus church facility that would allow it. A Catholic priest was one of the main speakers. The conference ended with Communion celebrated by him and another speaker, a Protestant. I believed that the only true unity Christians could ever experience would somehow involve the power of the Holy Spirit.

Before long, we were meeting regularly in the home of a former Florida State professor of music. His son, Herman Gunther, was a good friend having spent a good deal of his time with us at His Place. It was to this home church that Don Odon came. Don is a Hungarian evangelist and fearless Bible smuggler who has been jailed countless times by the authorities in eastern Europe. He frequented our meetings at the Gunthers and ministered in the power of God. Our little group was deeply touched by his stories of our counterparts in the Communist world. Because of him, and some young evangelists from a little church in rural England, our little home meeting became a world church—at least in its thinking.

In the summer of 1970, in what I now realize was an act of monumental faith and love, my parents sent me to Europe for two months. It was a summer of finding more of the pieces of the puzzle of what I felt God wanted in a church, and especially, what he wanted in me.

I spent a weekend at L'Abri, Francis Schaeffer's youth community in Switzerland, working, and learning that (1) everyone in the church contributes something, (2) that the church is the intellectual powerhouse for the world, and (3) in it the world should be able to find the truth that will set it free.

While visiting England, I found, in the tiny hamlet of South Chard in county Devon, what I believed to be a working model of the local church. In this amazing community of farmers and shepherds, ordinary church members were regularly sent out, after a few years of training and work locally, with a one-way plane ticket to wherever God called them. They were to encourage, and plant churches as they went, depending entirely on God for their daily needs and for their way back. Several ladies had just returned from their years in Nepal, a country closed to formal missionaries and ordinarily hardened to the Gospel. They brought with them a song they had sung in their meetings, so that the believers in Nepal could be a source of encouragement to those in England. I remember thinking this was a switch—the mission reaching out to bless the sending church.

Even a world-class case of "traveler's distress" could not deter the grace of God, working through his church. In Aberystwyth, Wales, the Presbyterian minister, although he and his family had to be away, generously lent me his home, the manse, and arranged for someone to look in on me regularly. I was neither British nor Presbyterian but he knew I was a Christian as was he.

That was all that mattered. For his great faith in God, his willingness to take in a young stranger from America but, especially for his bathroom, I am forever in his debt. This experience confirmed for me that the church should be the place where extraordinary grace meets extraordinary need across all artificial boundaries.

While in Europe, I also visited the evangelical convent and monastery in Darmstadt, Germany, built with rubble from World War II. This center of Bible- and literature-smuggling activity, founded by Klara (Mother Basilea) Schlink, was a haven of quiet. I was invited to join the monastery and to begin a life of both hard work and contemplation. I declined and moved on, but with a new understanding for and appreciation of the monastic life. Not only did they love one another, but they managed to do it while living together.

Then, for two glorious weeks in Czechoslovakia and Hungary I shared my faith freely with Odon's contacts. Ironically, it was in a place where believers at the time were less free than anywhere else on earth. These were my first attempts at public speaking. Fortunately, my interpreters were better speakers than I was and God blessed the listeners. But I was encouraged and edified by the experience.

Each experience left its mark on my life. I had been conditioned by my upbringing that constant change is normal and basically a good thing. In all my experience thus far the church had been a place of exciting, entertaining Bible teaching, not a fixed institution concerned with internal politics.

During my summer in Europe, I had learned several key lessons that prepared me for the shepherding movement. (1) Small-group church meetings in a home were places where one could experience the fullness of the presence of God like any other church. (2) There is only one church in a city consisting of all Christians.

(3) Christianity is a radical commitment of all of life to the cause of Christ. (4) The church ministers both to itself and to the world in the same miracle-working power of Jesus. (5) Fellowship of all kinds of believers is possible in the power of the Holy Spirit. (6) Church is a community where everyone contributes something; where each community recognizes and sends out its own ministers. (7) Christians in all countries can contribute to the church at large. (8) Denominational or national backgrounds have no bearing on acceptance of fellow Christians. (9) Christianity is a communal experience of being radically submitted to the Christian community's general good and its outreach to the world.

I returned to Tallahassee and my final year at Florida State that fall of 1970, more determined than ever to be part of a church that was on the cutting edge of what God is doing in the earth today.

Derek Prince returned to Tallahassee for more meetings. I no longer remember the topics he preached on but, at one of those meetings, I briefly met one of the girls I had prayed for two years earlier.

VICKI

Vicki grew up Waukeenah, Florida, a community of less than 200 people—most of them her relatives. She graduated from high school with the same people she had met in kindergarten, and attended the same country Methodist church all her life. On the surface, at least, she appeared to have had the kind of childhood other children dream about.

But suddenly, at age eleven, her fragile world collapsed. Her father was killed in an automobile accident. Only two weeks earlier, her grandfather, the family patriarch, had died of cancer. With the death of her father and grandfather, her mother had to join the work force and family life changed forever.

As her teen years progressed, Vicki's struggles with both the loss of her father and other personal issues compounded the stresses of adolescence. After graduating from high school in 1969, she attended a summer session at a junior college and got caught up in the drinking and drug culture. After a year of this self-destructive behavior, she decided that it was time to get her life together, but, try as she would, she was unable to do so. A new start seemed to be the only way out, and she began the enlistment process for training as an Army M.A.S.H nurse.

A few days later, on July 16, 1970, she attended church in her home town where the guest speaker was Tommy Cotton, a new graduate of Asbury Theological Seminary. He was fresh from the famous revival that had begun the previous February 3 on the Asbury college campus. His enthusiasm for the gospel was life to Vicki's spirit. She went to the altar knowing that she would forever be committing her life to the Lord. The army would have to make do with one less nurse.

At a youth retreat in August Vicki received the baptism of the Holy Spirit and started what she believed would be a lifelong journey with God. Tommy Cotton continued to fellowship with her over the next several weeks and introduced her to other Christians in Tallahassee whose faith seemed to be on fire. One of those Christians was Gerrit Gustafson.

Fresh from her new experiences with God, Vicki gushed with enthusiasm that autumn night after Derek Prince's meeting in the community room at the bank. As a "seasoned" Christian of nearly three years, I was pleased, but not impressed. In light of what God had in store for us in the future, that encounter with Vicki was definitely not love at first sight—I later found that the lack of feelings was mutual.

VIDEO MINISTRIES

I was in town for only a few weeks when a friend made a contact for me that would set the course of my life for years to come. Herman Gunther had graduated from Florida State the previous spring and had gone to be discipled for ministry at Bayview Heights Baptist Church in Mobile, Alabama. Charles Simpson, a popular speaker at Full Gospel Business Men's conventions was the pastor there. Herman had managed to set up an interview for me with Bob Mumford who was going to be preaching at Bayview in early January while Charles was away in New Zealand. I had heard of Mumford and had been impressed by his book *Fifteen Steps Out*. Mumford was beginning a new venture called Video Ministries, and since I was majoring in theater and taking courses in television, Herman figured that I would be interested.

After a successful interview and a miraculous series of events, I became the first student at Florida State to intern in his minor field of study, Television and Mass Communications. Early in the spring of my senior year, 1971, I found myself in Fort Lauderdale building a production truck and later helping operate it in Washington, D.C.

The vision for this new ministry was simple. I was to help make videotapes of the four Bible teachers for playback on videocassette in home prayer meetings. Prince, Simpson, Mumford, and Basham were in great demand as conference speakers and they figured that television would be able to extend their ministries into places where they would not be able to go in person.

The catch was it was 1971 and the videocassette was just a Japanese engineer's dream. The smallest video players were the size of a small refrigerator, cost a quarter of a million dollars, and required the expertise of a full-time technician for operation. Today it is easy to appreciate the vision of these men, but at the time, they were part of the only religious group in the world interested enough in videocassette technology to attend its first technical convention.

Within six weeks the production truck was finished, and we drove it from Fort Lauderdale, where the ministry was headquartered, to Washington, D.C. There, we spent another six weeks taping the teachers. We all, teachers and crew, lived in a borrowed apartment in a glorious celebration of community.

After the taping, Bob Mumford suggested to me, that since he was not accepting disciples and because I wanted to be discipled for the ministry, I might want to go Mobile to Charles Simpson's intern house for his disciples. I willingly agreed. However, because of Charles Simpson's heavy travel schedule, I spent a frustrating summer reading and studying in Mobile virtually on my own. Thus, I welcomed the opportunity to go with Video Ministries to Pittsburgh in the fall.

There I discovered that over the summer, a group of young pastors and evangelists had gathered in Fort Lauderdale to be discipled by Bob Mumford. Since I was not already in the ministry, I was not eligible to join the group. The time of working with and listening to the teachers in Pittsburgh was valuable, but I sensed I had missed the training opportunity of a lifetime by not being able to participate in Bob Mumford's discipleship group.

I was too "spiritual," though, to admit the rejection that I felt. Eager to obey the "man of God," I went back to Tallahassee at Mumford's suggestion, to embrace whatever ministry I could, with the understanding that I would later be able to return to Fort Lauderdale to be discipled by the first generation of his disciples. I had the feeling I was falling through the cracks. However, at the same time, I was continuously bathed in the teaching that every Christian ought to be submitted to some form of "covering." I was trying, but kept being refused. Each time I was refused, though, I was more convinced than ever of the great humility of these men of God and my need for their oversight.

Gerrit Gustafson, one of my roommates from college, had been discipled with Herman Gunther at the intern house in Mobile. He had returned to Tallahassee and had started a ministry house in Tallahassee called The Good Word. The Jesus People movement was at its height and houses like these were common in most major cities. I had lived there briefly before my internship with Video Ministries. That fall of 1971, I rejoined him and in spite of our complete lack of professional training, God used us as we practiced what the four teachers had taught us. We saw many people delivered from lives of immorality and drug use through encouragement, Bible teaching, and constant Christian fellowship. Few we ministered to were hard-core addicts. Most were students suffering from the spiritual oppression that accompanies heavy drug use. They tended to get better just by living with other Christians after a personal conversion experience.

We observed that depression was often a problem for those who experimented with a combination of eastern meditation and hallucinogens. One man in particular suffered bouts of severe depression. He had become a Christian, but still suffered greatly. Late one night, he felt so bad he couldn't sleep, and came to my room to talk. Half-asleep, but wanting to help, I said to him, "You just need to dance before the Lord."

"What? I feel like crying, not dancing."

"Just go ahead," I said earnestly, falling back asleep. Right then, in the hallway, came the sound of big feet on the hardwood floor. Boom! Boom! Boom! Of course, I hadn't meant for him to dance right then, late the next morning would have been fine.

Before I could wake up enough to stop him, he began to shout. "Yippee! Praise the Lord!"

Instantly, all the lights in the house came on (as well as most of them on our block). Only then could we tell the strange sounds he was making were shouts of joy. A brief celebration ensued, and I remember falling asleep that night thinking that it must have been his simple obedience that had brought about his deliverance.

We had learned the ministry of deliverance from Don Basham and Derek Prince, leaders who had related themselves with Charles Simpson and Bob Mumford. We had watched them firsthand at conferences and had learned from them just like Jesus' disciples had learned from him. God was faithful to deliver the oppressed in spite of our youth and exuberance.

But Bobby Renn, an old friend and former Florida State football teammate of Burt Reynolds, reminded us we were amateurs. Bobby was an alcoholic, and in spite of all our teaching, fellowship, and deliverance ministry, he could never stay sober for more than a few months at a time. He died sitting alone in his car by the side of a road. The cause of death was multiple organ damage as a result of his alcoholism.

We had not been the only ones to minister to him, of course. When we met him, he had already been through the alcohol-treatment system countless times. But we felt we should have succeeded where the system had failed— especially since we were supposed to have been ministering in the power of God. We felt we had lost both a battle and a good friend because we lacked the proper "equipment."

An experience in the Holy Spirit and a little discipling had gotten us this far. We reasoned that deeper experiences and more radical discipling must be what we needed. Maybe we could have helped Bobby if we had known how to disciple him. Gerrit then moved to Fort Lauderdale with Charles Simpson to live in his home and to become his personal assistant. I took over the leadership of the Good Word temporarily. I considered myself under the discipling of Bob Mumford, and waited to move to Fort Lauderdale.

PARTNERS IN LIFE AND MINISTRY

I was beginning to feel very comfortable being single and serving God in the house ministry and at my job with the fellowship duplicating and mailing teaching cassettes. After Gerrit left, God sent Vicki Buzbee, a good secretary, an understanding prayer partner, and a friend. No one in our fellowship saw our relationship as being anything else.

During her first year and a half in the fellowship in Tallahassee, Vicki's enthusiasm for the Lord and sense of humor provided her with many opportunities to share her testimony at various churches and Full Gospel Business Men's meetings. She was also leading the women's house ministry. Several of the girls were engaged, and Vicki felt frustrated because God had not brought someone into her life. Marriage seemed far away and she found herself slipping into a deep depression. She wanted to marry a man who would put God first in his life, but her former life, filled as it had been with male companionship, haunted her. When it seemed she might lose her way, she found herself, one midnight, in the chapel of the old downtown Presbyterian church. There she decided she wanted the Lord more than a husband and made a vow to serve Him, married or not.

One night, following her decision, we were praying together after a fellowship dinner as was our custom and I had what I can only describe as a vision. In my vision two gold bricks (representing Vicki and me) were resting on the third step of a golden platform. I couldn't see what was on the platform because of the bright light. Without difficulty, I lifted the bricks with my foot, step by step, until they reached the top level. Instantly, they disappeared. Vicki sighed heavily, and I heard that the offering of our lives and ministries had been accepted by God. I remember praying, "What do you mean 'our' lives and ministries?" The vision ended. I told Vicki what I had seen and she "saw" it too.

I didn't tell Vicki about the "our lives" part, and we spent the next three days, as the implications slowly dawned on us studiously ignoring the vision and each other as best we could. Finally, out of sheer frustration, she said, "Well what do you think God is saying?" I said, without a hint of emotion, "I think the Lord wants us to be married." Vicki's answer to this thoroughly unromantic proposal was a shaky, "I think you're right," and we found ourselves engaged to be married. We had never dated and did not feel at all in love, but believed God was calling us together and we were determined to obey his will.

Suddenly, almost everyone in our fellowship seemed to share the vision, and communicated that they just knew it was right. Love came quickly, but we have always said ours was an "arranged" marriage. After the custom portrayed in the then-current movie, *Fiddler on the Roof*, our wedding feast was on March 18, 1972, at a Tallahassee hotel. Gerrit Gustafson married us and we used vows written weeks earlier by Charles Simpson that better expressed our new views on the nature of marriage than did the traditional vows. Because of the nature of our wedding, the hotel management assumed ours was a Jewish wedding.

Vicki and I were married about the same time as four other couples our age. We had all been residents of the ministry houses before we were married. We were all part of a growing fellowship that met in the back room of a carpet shop. We saw each other almost daily and met together for prayer and Bible study at least weekly. Close, personal experiences were what we expected church to be about, but we always felt that eventually we would move to Fort Lauderdale.

The next two years of our lives were spent on a "seesaw." Leaders in the fellowships in Tallahassee and Fort Lauderdale were called elders and they expected that members in the fellowship who were serious about following God would submit themselves to elder oversight. The elders felt responsible to help us find the will of God, but when the leaders of our fellowship in Tallahassee would release us to move to Fort Lauderdale we were told the leadership there did not feel the time was right, and vice versa. For us to have moved when either group was not favorable would have implied that we were rebellious.

During this two-year period, we attended several conferences in Fort Lauderdale and developed friendships in the fellowship there. Finally, Bob Mumford in Fort Lauderdale admitted that he was not able to give the time he thought necessary to disciple me, and suggested I look to one of his disciples. Reluctantly we agreed and attended a discipling meeting at Tom and Gwen Monroe's house. Eventually, both sets of leaders were agreeable to us moving, and we made a job and house hunting trip. I found a job, and an apartment near other members of the fellowship in Fort Lauderdale. We returned to Tallahassee on a Sunday to pack and move to Fort Lauderdale, grateful that we were finally going to be discipled.

Monday morning at my office, I began to feel uncomfortable about what was happening. When I got home for lunch, I said to Vicki, "You won't believe what I think God is saying to me." Immediately she answered,

"I don't know about you, but all morning I've been feeling we're not supposed to go to Fort Lauderdale." After two years of "knowing" God's will, everything had changed. We sheepishly told the elders, that now that they approved, we would not be moving.

A few months before, our friend Gerrit had been sent to Monte Vista, Colorado. A growing fellowship there had asked Charles Simpson to move there and lead them. Simpson declined, but had sent Gerrit to minister in his place. Gerrit's initiation into the ministry had come about after he had watched Simpson at conferences and had served in his home. In essence Simpson had discipled him. Gerrit offered to prepare and send me out to minister in the same way.

Finally, I was on track to be approved and sent out for ministry. I jumped at the opportunity. Since reading Howard Butt's *The Velvet Covered Brick*, even knowing I would now be submitting to a friend did not bother me. *The Velvet Covered Brick* tells the story of an older brother who thought his submission to his younger brother was God's way of teaching him true humility. I couldn't argue with that. It made perfect sense to me.

After years of waiting, our adventure in discipleship had finally begun. We were ready to do anything, willing to endure anything, and prepared to pay any personal price necessary to be part of a church we felt was on the cutting edge of what God was doing in the earth.

3

A GLIMPSE OF HEAVEN

ARRIVAL IN COLORADO, FELLOWSHIP

Upon our arrival in Colorado, we found a church that was a fellowship of families. Small groups met weekly in the homes and everyone came together for a large meeting once a month. The church had no building, but met in a borrowed conference room of a potato processing warehouse owned by one of the members. The lack of a building, or permanent meeting place was planned. Membership was a matter of relationship, not ritual—it was not by confession of faith, or transfer of letter, but by declaration of intent to be discipled by one of the leaders. As members, we were accountable to one of the two full-time pastors and they were both directly accountable to Charles Simpson.

Many of the men of our church worked together, their families ate meals together frequently, and they shared their lives on a daily basis. The praise and worship they experienced at each weekly meeting was like what we had seen only at large conventions. The combination of high praise and close fellowship was the summation of all we believed the church should be and the small, isolated, rural town of Monte Vista only intensified the experience.

AS UNTO THE LORD, SERVING

When a church learns to serve, enormous resources become available. No one in our church ever had to go through anything alone. Through illness, bereavement, and all the other ups and downs of life the group was always there. Women shared cleaning chores, and provided free babysitting for each other. Single women provided free babysitting that allowed harried couples to have a night out. Men helped each other with home repairs and yard work. We did not use our garage in the summer so we lent it to a member who had started a saw-sharpening business. Illnesses or new babies meant that after the family went home there would be ongoing help with meals and house cleaning. Church members could find a job or emergency financial help through the church. Some of the more mechanically inclined gave themselves to keeping cars fixed. Single women and the elderly had minor maintenance checks performed on their cars automatically.

There was always provision for emergencies. Someone always had a trailer to help bring a crippled car home for repairs. When Vicki had to be hospitalized for fainting spells, a motor home was provided for me to take her to Colorado Springs, and a nurse who was a member of the fellowship volunteered to go along to tend to her. My pastor made a hospital call over two hundred miles from his home to both pray with us and to pay the entire week's hospital bill out of church funds because we had no insurance. When I lost my job a few months after arriving in Colorado, the church provided for us all winter until I could get a job in the spring. Our new environment seemed like heaven on earth.

The church was a place of guaranteed friends and instant family. Within weeks, I became "Uncle Ronnie" to "Uncle Gerry's" kids. We didn't have to work at establishing close relationships with loving, caring people. Friendships were an outgrowth of the fellowship. We felt instantly accepted. We began to believe that we were going to be friends with these people for life.

Because pastors served by leading, there was constant, rich Bible teaching. They were never content to just bring a message, but provided spiritual food for the church. Sermons often lasted over an hour and a half. Each message was more like a seminar, and everyone took copious notes.

The leaders of the church in the book of Acts said in Acts 6:1–4 it would not be right for them to neglect the ministry of the Word to "wait on tables." It didn't seem right to us for our leaders to mow their own grass or care for their own cars when they could better use the time to minister the Word. Their wives also ministered, spending much of the day praying and sharing with other women, and they could often be found cooking or cleaning for someone who was sick. We felt they should not have to stop to wash clothes or clean bathrooms. So, the church members cared for the mundane things in their leaders' lives like lawn mowing and cleaning. We felt that by doing these things for our leaders and their families we were doing them as "unto the Lord." Serving them was a joy! The story of David and his mighty men who risked their lives to get a drink for him from Bethlehem's well was told often. We felt we knew the love and loyalty that must have motivated David's men. It became an honor to be able to honor those in authority. Our service to them was service to the Lord Jesus himself. As for myself, I felt I was learning how to serve the Lord better, and that's what really mattered. As for Vicki, she was learning better ways to keep our house, honor her husband, and raise our children.

THE SALT OF THE COVENANT, LOYALTY

Salt naturally sticks to itself. We have to add chemicals or use other means in order to get it to flow freely. Sand, on the other hand, has no such cohesion, and naturally tends to separate into individual grains. As Christians, we are the salt of the earth, and when salt looses its saltiness, it is useless. "Covenant loyalty," as we called it, was a part of the identity of the Christian—a visible characteristic that distinguishes the Christian from the world. Christians should be like salt, not sand, and should stick together. A Christian who lost his loyalty was like salt that had lost its saltiness. In our church community, we were members of one another, and loyal to each other. For us, loyalty was a natural part of being a Christian. When you know you are friends for life, you stick together, you overlook the little things, and you are loyal!

Because of loyalty to one another, gossip was forbidden. You couldn't reveal another's secrets or problems without being disloyal to them. In this environment, we all felt complete trust in each other. If we had a question about someone's attitude or behavior, it was considered a matter of personal integrity to trust that person's pastor to handle the situation.

On the home front, we were frequently defending our church and its leaders to our parents, other family, and past friends. Their lack of understanding of how our church family functioned offered us many opportunities to express how wonderful the close-knit group of people were. We were able to easily contrast our church with the ones they participated in.

The Christian life was an everyday experience of life

in Monte Vista, not just a Sunday morning ritual. We had moved there for the biblical way of preparation for the ministry, discipleship. I would be discipled by Gerrit, now our pastor, to lead and care for a group like the one we were part of. Then, in a year or two, I would be sent out, just as Paul and Barnabas had been in Acts 13, and just as Gerrit had been months before.

After eighteen months, Gerrit "felt led" to move to Pascagoula, Mississippi. Charles Simpson had moved there from Fort Lauderdale and had started a church. Gerrit wanted an on-going relationship with Simpson as his permanent personal pastor. Until that time, Charles Simpson had been Gerrit's temporary disciple-maker. Since we felt called to be discipled by Gerrit, we really had no other reason to stay in Colorado. Most of the other men being discipled by him decided to leave their careers and continue their discipling relationship. In a few years, the other pastor from Colorado felt the same need (to be discipled by Simpson) and almost thirty families ended up moving to the Gulf coast.

The church in Mississippi was far larger than the one in Monte Vista had been, but it had many of the same personal touches we had loved so much in Colorado. We felt that maybe, in a larger church, God would open an opportunity for me to be sent out in ministry.

We found a higher intensity of serving in Mississippi than we had known in Colorado. People willingly sacrificed their time and energy in order to serve. The reason for this intensity was, that a few months before, several of the men of the church had temporarily been laid off at the shipyard. About the same time, another man's construction business had slowed down. Although he was falling behind in his payments, he still owned a large sailboat that had been a colorful part of Gulf coast history, and that he was restoring. Foreclosure would have meant not only the loss of his investment in the boat, but also his business. The church was able to purchase the yacht, a gracious, sixty-seven-foot staysail schooner, for what the businessman owed, and hired him to lead a team of laid-off shipyard workers to finish the restoration. As a result, his business was saved and everyone continued to receive a paycheck. We jokingly called the schooner our "educational building" during the restoration because of the many hard but valuable lessons learned by all who worked on it. (Owners, and especially former owners, of fine old wooden yachts will understand the education designation fully.) This conduct, "above and beyond the call of duty" for a church, earned for it the loyalty and total commitment of all its members. We fittingly rechristened the schooner *The Committed*.

Because we felt that a church should incorporate intense fellowship, serving, and loyalty in order to truly reflect Christ, we felt that we had finally found the fulfillment of everything we were looking for in a church. Opportunity for me to begin to minister the Word seemed far away now, but the fellowship and worship were so good that it didn't matter quite so much.

Our church was filled with warm, loving, open people—people willing to give themselves for others. Who wouldn't want to be part to a church like that?

4

THE PILLARS OF HEAVEN

Seven basic principles not practiced by most churches shaped the character and conduct of the churches that made up the shepherding movement. We will call them the Pillars of Heaven. Three of these principles, fellowship, service, and loyalty were addressed in the last chapter. The other four, authority, tithing, place of natural things, and God's order of the home, are presented in this chapter. If you have never been part of a church like the one described in the last chapter, please remember that we had, in front of us, a church producing some very good fruit that believed and practiced these principles.

AUTHORITY

Kingdom Authority

Throughout the history of the church tensions have arisen between Spirit and structure, institution and charisma. The modern charismatic movement has been characterized by its emphasis on the spiritual gifts, its freedom, and its lack of structure. This lack of structure has often led to serious character problems in Christians because the same freedom that permits the operation of the gifts of the Spirit also gives occasion to the flesh. The visible result was a gap between the espoused spirituality and the character of charismatics. This gap has sometimes been a wide one, undermining our Christian testimony. It should not exist. The shepherding movement was born as the result of an attempt to close the gap by emphasizing character building within the context of a charismatic fellowship.

The full message of the gospel combines power and character. The gospel should lead us beyond salvation for our souls and power for miracles. Is it enough to receive Christ as your Savior if he is not truly Lord? Does he have absolute rule over every conscious decision in every area of your life? . . . Every day? . . . Are you sure? A complete understanding of the gospel will bring believers into God's kingdom under his lordship. By receiving the gospel of the kingdom of God, believers place themselves under God's authority.

In the Old and New Testaments there are hundreds of instances where God's will in heaven breaks into history here on earth. The sun stood still, plagues came, and the Red Sea parted. God's people experienced unparalleled prosperity when they obeyed, poverty and destruction when they didn't.

In the New Testament, three thousand people were added to the church in a day. The lame walked, the blind received their sight, the deaf heard, and the dead were raised by the will of God. These things are described in the Gospels as the result of the nearness of the kingdom or reign of God.

Delegated Authority

The common thread in all these accounts is the presence of a mediator. Whether by Moses, David,

Solomon, the army of the Assyrians, Jesus, Peter, or Paul, God has always accomplished his will on earth through intermediaries. As the King of heaven and earth, he delegates his authority on earth to men. Jesus was the perfect example of God's delegated authority. The Father's authority was and is forever delegated to the Son. In the Incarnation, the Father's authority was manifested on earth by the obedient Son, Jesus. He further delegated his authority to his disciples as seen in Matthew 10:1 and again in Matthew 28:18. In Acts, we find this delegation extended after the Resurrection to the disciples and followers of Jesus for the purpose of fulfilling the Great Commission.

The Personal Pastor

Many Christian leaders today point out that the command of the Great Commission is not just to make converts. In Matthew 28:18–19 Jesus says, "All authority in heaven and on earth has been given to me. Therefore go and make disciples of all nations. . . ." Jesus' authority is associated with making disciples. Jesus made disciples by using the authority that was delegated to him by the Father. Similarly, we are commanded to make disciples by the authority Christ has delegated to us. Our task is not complete, though, until our disciples are able to make disciples themselves.

The most visible form of that delegated authority in the shepherding movement is the personal pastor, or disciple-maker. The writer of Hebrews commands his readers, as we see in chapter 13, verse 17, to "Obey your leaders and submit to their authority." To explain this admonition he says, "They keep watch over you as men who must give an account." With authority comes responsibility. Pastors and leaders must answer to God for the conduct and character of their followers.

Most pastors in the movement take their responsibilities very seriously. If they must give an account for the conduct of their followers, then, logically, they feel that followers must demonstrate some willingness to obey before they can risk taking them on as a responsibility. Willingness on the part of the follower to obey is called "teachableness." This may mean anything from a simple commitment to follow the example of the leader, to moving, either across town or across the country. Sometimes, though, committing to meet regularly is all that is involved.

A follower who confesses a problem in a particular area, say the handling of finances, should submit the problem to the oversight of the pastor in order for the pastor to have "entrance" into this area of the follower's life and for discipling to begin. This commitment is the follower's literal "joint" to the visible manifestation of the body of Christ. Through this joint, all the supply of Christ and his church is available to meet the need. And through this joint, the lordship of Jesus Christ can be more fully realized in the daily life of the believer in practical, experiential ways. One man cannot effectively pastor more than ten or twelve men or single women in this way. Pastors do not disciple the wives of husbands who are "submitted" to them. The wives are thought of as being "pastored" by their husbands.

Commitment to a personal pastor is considered a serious matter. In the Bible, church leaders seemed to know the members of their group personally and were committed to their well-being. Jesus' commitment to his disciples cost him his life. The disciples' commitment to him and each other cost them their lives. There always will be a "cost" to true discipleship.

This committed relationship brings a great sense of security. There is the very real feeling, spiritually, of "coming in out of the rain." Those who share a commitment to the same pastor become close friends, and find commitment extending to one another. Because of this understanding, the greatest concern of church leadership is to help the new follower find his or her "place." That place in the body of Christ is not to be thought of in terms of ministry or service in the church. Finding your place means finding which pastor could best disciple you. Those who come into a "calling" are more interested in their own gifts and ministries rather than ministering to people. When they are discipled by the right person, God will then make room for the gift he has given the disciple in the context of community.

Life decisions

My pastor was always there as a sounding board for any leadings or impressions that I received from the Lord in personal prayer. The pastor is responsible for his followers' well-being in all areas of their lives. All large investments, like house and car purchases, have implications beyond just the individual and his family. If a follower makes a contract that he is unable to fulfill, or a purchase that is beyond his means, the pastor, and ultimately the entire church, stands to suffer financially. It is only fair that the pastor have real control over these decisions. My pastor once willingly gave a substantial amount of his family's inheritance to one of his disciples to help him out of a business problem. We were all, pastors and followers, looking for God's will.

Obedience

The most important standard of conduct for the disciple is obedience. Obedience to God and his Word, and to the delegated authority placed over him or her in the body of Christ is a sign of maturity and faith in God.

Obedience is always as unto the Lord. We do not obey just because what our pastor recommends is better or wiser than what we would have done. We obey with the full assurance that even if the pastor is wrong, God will "work all things together for our good," since our hearts are toward him. My pastor never seemed to direct or rebuke me in ways that I thought directly contradicted the Scriptures. Usually his counsel seemed to take the side of common sense.

KINGDOM TAXES

Tithing

Tithing, in our case the systematic giving of one-tenth of one's pre-tax income, is almost universal. The tithe, in the form of a check made out to the church, is given directly to one's personal pastor. We felt this a more biblical means of giving, since in the Old Testament the tithe went to the priests. Thus, those whose sole inheritance is from their ministry received the tithe. Tithing in this way is very personal—our tithe didn't just go into a collection plate, it went into someone's hand.

All tithes then passed through the church account, where they were tallied, audited, and accounted for at the end of the year with a receipt. Pastors are paid a salary based on the total of the tithes collected. This is a very practical system. The pastor makes an average of what his people make. Since the most he could be expected to effectively pastor in the way described above is ten to twelve families, I knew exactly where my money went. There were no denominational assessments and no building maintenance.

Over and above the tithe, there is also what is known as the "pilgrimage offering," named after the Old Testament practice of saving one-third of a tithe for pilgrimages to Jerusalem. This offering is not given to the church, but saved for conference attendance expenses. Other offerings include benevolence offerings for those in the church who had need, various love offerings to support the visits of occasional guest speakers, special gifts for pastors, and special offerings to support *New Wine Magazine* or to buy property and eventually to build buildings.

Tithes were jokingly called "Kingdom Taxes" and only money exceeding the tithe was considered to be offerings. Giving was one way that resources were transferred from the "natural realm" to the "spiritual realm."

THE PLACE OF NATURAL THINGS

First the Natural, Then the Spiritual

Full-time vocational Christian service is viewed as a promotion. The term "ministry" is not used since the biblical equivalent of the word is service. All serving is called ministry. The idea of an individual being "called to minister" is not accepted since it is understood we are all "called out of darkness" to be "the people of God," (1 Pet. 2:9–10), and to live lives that cause the pagans to glorify God. All Christians are called to minister. The designations of "lay" and "clergy" are not biblical in origin.

Serving as a full-time pastor or leader of a small group is not considered a calling. It is a great honor that can only be attained by both obvious gifting and "faithfulness in natural things."

The Natural-Spiritual Connection

The natural realm and the spiritual realm are connected—both are created by God. According to 1 Corinthians 15:46, we find them graded. "The spiritual did not come first, but the natural, and after that the spiritual."

The natural is first; the spiritual, last. One must pass grade one before going on to grade two. Since the natural is first, faithfulness in secular matters must proceed any endeavor in spiritual matters.

Diligence and success in natural things demonstrate one's potential for faithfulness in spiritual things. Diligence and success on the job, and excellence in sports when at play, indicate fitness in a follower's walk with God. Conversely, a lack of success on the job, or lack of dedication in sports, is a possible sign of a poor relationship with God.

Productivity

Faithfulness can be a difficult commodity to measure, but measuring productivity is easy. The ability to get results is a handy measure of faithfulness. I had a vegetable garden when we lived in Colorado. The soil there is rich, but at 7,600 feet of elevation there were only ninety days between frosts. With a growing season that short having just a pretty garden was nothing to be proud of. The garden had to be worthwhile, and if the garden was to be worthwhile, everything had to produce, and produce quickly or be frozen. In the shepherding movement, getting results is the objective—in gardening, sports, on the job, or in ministry.

The biblical parables of sowing and reaping are clearly about the importance of getting results. Results are the measure of the person who is a doer of the word, not just a hearer, and indicate (1) a diligence to sow, (2) the fitness of the heart of the sower, and (3) the worthiness of the endeavor. Productivity is the standard for evaluation of every aspect of a follower's life.

Natural maturity occurs when a child, through work, produces more resources than it consumes. Spiritual maturity happens when followers produce more in terms of spiritual ministry to others than they receive from their pastor. In the maturing process there will be fewer and fewer things in the follower's life that require the pastor's attention.

GOD'S ORDER IN THE HOME

The husband and father is to mediate Christ's "headship" in the home. He is the spiritual covering for the home. He is the spiritual watchman appointed by God to protect, nurture, and provide for his wife and children. He is God's delegated authority in the family. He is the family's pastor. As such, he is ultimately responsible for all aspects of home life.

Husbands, Love Your Wives

In Ephesians 5:25–26, we read, "Husbands, love your wives, just as Christ loved the church and gave himself up for her to make her holy, cleansing her by the washing with water through the word." According to this verse a husband is equipped to meet all his wife's spiritual needs. A husband is responsible for washing his wife as verse 26 commands. We interpreted this verse to mean that the husband is expected to be his wife's counselor and help her apply the Word to her life. Her husband covers her and the home spiritually.

The husband is responsible for the financial aspects of the home. He develops the budget, pays the bills, and balances the checkbook. In 1 Timothy 5:8 we read, "If anyone does not provide for his relatives, and especially for his immediate family, he has denied the faith and is worse than an unbeliever." Husbands are strongly encouraged to provide for their families in such a way that their wives do not have to work outside the home.

WIVES, SUBMIT YOURSELVES

In a world of failing families, our church encouraged a father to be strong and lead his family spiritually and physically. When a father is strong, wives and children feel secure. A wife learned, as the Living Bible translates it in 1 Peter 3:1, to "fit in" with her "husband's plans." Many leading Christian leaders agree that Ephesians 5 and 1 Peter 3:1 teach the submission of the wife to the husband, and that it is the cornerstone of the Christian family.

Children Obey Your Parents

A father is directly responsible for his children's education, conduct, and discipline. Children are a reflection of how well the father covers his household. In God's eyes, failure as a father means failure—regardless of any other successes. Proverbs 22:6 commands the father to "Train a child in the way he should go." A father usually accomplishes this by delegating his authority over the children to his wife. A wife brings major issues to her husband, whose decision is final. She is accountable to her husband for their children and children receive consistent discipline since they cannot play one parent against another. Such is the wisdom of God's order for the home.

Others

Single women are prepared for marriage by first living in a house or apartment with several other single women from the church. Later they might have the opportunity to live with an "adopted" family. Living with a real family gives them the opportunity to see firsthand how to run a household, care for children, and see how a Christian husband/wife relationship is supposed to function. Single men are expected to learn from their pastor the spiritual skills and physical diligence necessary to provide for and effectively lead a family.

PILLARS OF INTEGRITY

In a disintegrating society, where denominational churches seemed to be discarding their integrity, a strong Christian community of stable families with strong leadership seemed to be the foundation of the kingdom of God, and the extension of his rule on the earth. Insuring a disciple's integrity in the home, on the job, and in the church is the objective of these pillars of heaven.

When things got tough these seven pillars seemed to be all that would not be shaken. If they did not provide the comfort and security we felt we needed, we only had ourselves to blame. They were the word of God for our lives.

5

I'M SORRY, IT'S JUST NOT WORKING OUT

SEVEN PILLARS

Our version of the kingdom of heaven rested firmly on seven pillars, fellowship, serving, loyalty, authority, tithing, faithfulness in natural things, and order in the home. When they failed, the joy of living in a Christian community was replaced with the sting of rejection, and because of our trust in these principles we felt like it was all our fault.

The pastor-disciple relationship was supposed to be permanent, but if after a few years, the pastor wanted to make adjustments to his responsibilities, for whatever reason, he could. The so-called spiritual way out of a relationship was for the pastor to "humbly" admit that he had taken the follower as far as he could and that the continuation of the discipling process could be better overseen by another pastor. Ironically, this "other pastor" usually meant one of the other followers. In the hierarchy of authority, this was a demotion, pure and simple. No matter how spiritual you were, it hurt. One of your friends and co-laborers would now be your pastor.

CHANGES

In 1979 we began to suspect that, with so many new people coming in, there would be a shifting around of some of our pastor's followers to other men. The practice was known as "re-relating." We would have light conversations with our friends about the changes we knew were coming for some of us. We had been with our pastor for five years at this time and friends of his for several years before that. Although our relationship was not as intimate as we desired, we did not expect a change for ourselves. However, each of us wondered who would "make the cut."

The changes began when Gerrit asked one of his men, a former Baptist pastor, to begin to look for discipling to another of his men. Though we had been good friends with this former pastor, we no longer saw one another as often, and eventually saw one another only at large meetings. This man's new pastor was outgoing and sincere, but was not as formally trained or experienced as was the man he was supposed to be discipling. Both tried their best, but eventually, the re-related brother and his family moved away.

Our dear friend and beloved physician was next. He had left a successful medical practice in Colorado to move to Mobile to continue to be "pastored" by Gerrit. Eventually, he felt that since they were not making sufficient progress in their discipleship, it would be best for them to re-relate to one of Gerrit's men. The feelings of personal rejection that inevitably followed such a change were mixed with a sense of relief. The relationship that had brought so much joy had become a source of great frustration.

But the way the "system" worked caused other pain. Their children felt rejected and isolated from the other children in our group. The family's time was spent trying to form relationships in their new context and our time was divided among those left in our group. We rarely saw them again.

Our pastor, himself, was re-related. Gerrit had once been pastored by Charles Simpson. In fact, he had been one of his first disciples. But now he had been re-related to another of Charles Simpson's men, and generally testified that the change had been greatly beneficial. However, being re-related was humiliating, painful, and not generally fruitful. One divorced woman I talked to years later remarked that to be re-related to another pastor felt exactly the same as going through a divorce.

FAILING TO MAKE THE CUT

My pastor called to have a meeting with me. This always meant bad news, since pastors never called their followers just for fellowship. (It was our job to pursue them.) As I left for the meeting, Vicki saw me off with a deep sense of fear. When I returned I didn't have to tell her the news. It was written on my face.

Gerrit released himself from being my pastor. He said that he had brought me as far as he could in my spiritual life and it was time for someone else to step in. He still felt responsible for me, and suggested that one of three other men pastored by him might be that someone else. Of course, this begged the question, "If you couldn't do it what makes you think they can?" But I was too "spiritual" to ask that. Actually, I couldn't say anything. It felt like being fired from a job or losing a good friend in a car accident. The sense of loss was so total that I could only respond in empty platitudes.

As I shared the news with Vicki, she sat on the floor in our son's room and wept. How could this possibly be happening to us. We had entered into a "covenant" with my pastor believing that the relationship would be for life.

We felt personally rejected by him. And it was personal. All our friends were in his group. We, as a couple, had felt joined to Gerrit and his wife for eternity. Losing him as our pastor meant not only losing his friendship, but it also essentially meant losing our closest friends, since most of them were "relating" to him. Our being re-related meant having to start all over. We were not sure that we would ever be able to give ourselves to friends again.

ETERNAL RELATIONSHIPS?

We thought that a major advantage of covenant communities was the sense that our relationships were permanent. These were the people that we would be in fellowship with for the rest of our lives. There was something very secure about having a core group of people who would always be there for you. Of course there would be new people coming in, but there would always be that inner circle of friends. It was fun to look to the future and wonder whose kids would marry whom, and how much fun it would be to grow old together.

We felt like we were spiritual "marines" taking new ground for the kingdom. After all, what we were doing was on the cutting edge and not everyone would be comfortable there. It was no shame to feel the need to leave. Anyone who couldn't make it was "washed out" in love. Like David's men in 1 Samuel 30:23, we were told that those who did not "cross over" with us still deserved their share of the "spoils." Of course, the implication was that the one leaving was somehow not measuring up, and had to be left behind to "guard the baggage."

SEARCHING FOR A REASON

Because we had been re-related, we would now be guarding the baggage. We were not quitting, we had been fired. During the days that followed, I searched within myself for the real reason as to why I had been cut. Maybe if I had been able to make some disciples of my own this would not have happened. But the one man I had been sharing with was not interested in joining our church. He had wonderfully renewed his relationship with the Lord, but he was not interested in being discipled as we were. I just was not "producing" new people. Then again, maybe if my business had been doing better, or if only I had gotten that new job, I would not have been cut.

Vicki who had finally begun to feel close to my pastor's wife, Himmie, faced the loss of a relationship that was important to her. Then, she began to feel like she had not measured up. What more could she have done to help insure we would not be re-related? How had she failed to live up to the standard for a godly wife. I had been dishonored and it was a reflection on her.

Eventually I stopped looking for a reason and accepted the shame. I began to think that this must be God's will and started to search for a new pastor. The three men Gerrit had recommended were friends and I was far too proud to be discipled by them. I viewed that as a demotion.

THE CHOICE

One of Gerrit's new responsibilities was Noel Timmerman, the leader of a small home church in Jacksonville, Florida. His group had grown to over twenty families and was, in our view, more than one man could effectively pastor. Gerrit told me that Noel could probably use some help in dividing his group into two care groups. Nothing more was said about this by him or Noel, but the implication was that I was to help in the process. Gerrit and I made a trip to Jacksonville and met briefly with Noel about my re-relating to him. I got the first job I interviewed for and made preparations to move.

In the intervening weeks before my arrival in Jacksonville, however, conditions changed in Noel's group. Four of the men being discipled by him were made leaders of their own small groups. By the time we arrived, the main reason for my coming had disappeared. Noel and his family had been invited to spend the summer in Mobile, and he temporarily re-related me to one of his men.

It was a time of real uncertainty for us. We had a new baby, a new home, and new group of "eternal relationships" to build. We resolved to try to give ourselves again.

The fact was, I had been rejected again. When Noel returned at the end of the summer, we still did not know exactly where we fit. Noel was my pastor, but because I did not have anyone that I was discipling, I was not included in the meetings Noel had with his four leaders. We were meeting with one of his follower's groups, just for fellowship, but not really building any ties with Noel or his followers and their families.

Vicki was feeling more and more confused about her place. She was asked to serve at luncheons for the leader's wives. This was actually the group she was a part of—except when they were meeting as wives of the leadership. She felt very humiliated and at the same time, berated herself for her lack of humility.

Gerrit and Himmie visited the Timmerman's that fall. Although we both felt something was not right we could say nothing to them without, in our minds, dishonoring Noel. Even though Vicki was close to Himmie she could not share our problems with her or ask her to pray for her since that would be uncovering me as her husband and Noel as my pastor. The whole visit was a time of walking on eggshells, trying to figure out how to fit in with this new fellowship.

VISION

Shortly after arriving in Jacksonville, while crossing one of its many bridges I had a vision. I saw myself at the Last Judgment. It was not a terrifying experience. Jesus had already interceded on my behalf, and the questions were not directed at my sin. The questions were about the things I had not done in his name when the opportunities had presented themselves. I don't recall the specific instance in question, but I do recall my answer—I hadn't done that certain thing because my pastor had said it wasn't a good idea.

Gently it occurred to me that it was not my pastor who was having to give an account for what I had failed to do, but me. I said, "But what about Hebrews 13:17, 'Obey those who have rule over you and submit yourselves, for they watch for your souls, as those who will have to give an account.'" I then recalled that the verse says "*as* those who will have to give an account," not "*since* they have to give an account." Another believer's responsibility to God for me is very limited. My lack of obedience to God's leading was not excused just because my pastor discouraged me. I had to give an account for my disobedience and he had to give account for his.

I REJECT MY PASTOR

With this understanding, I finally met with Noel in December, and explained that I felt unable to follow as I should and asked to be released to find another pastor. He agreed that the relationship was not working, and released me.

Within a week, the phone stopped ringing and our

friends were no longer available for dinner. Church meetings, which were not regular, went by without our knowing about them, and soon almost all communication ceased. Vicki asked Noel's wife if she could continue cleaning at her home. These times of service had been her only source of social interaction and fellowship. She went several times, but the ladies didn't initiate any conversations with her and she decided that it was just too hard. After eight years of very close church relationships we were suddenly isolated and on our own in a strange town. We were, in fact, being shunned. The other members of the group felt we wanted nothing to do with them because we had rejected their pastor.

Ironically, a few days after our meeting, Noel decided that his relationship with Gerrit was not working and went back relating to his former pastor. Nothing changed for him socially. He seemed to continue pastoring his group as if nothing had happened.

SIX WEEKS OF PAIN

I handled the situation by exercising "great spirituality"—I denied it and gave myself to my job determined to find fulfillment in my new career in professional video-equipment sales.

Vicki was not so "spiritual." I tried to help her see that this was all in God's plan for us, but, not surprisingly, she slipped into a deep depression. For the first time in our marriage I didn't have the answers for her and she had no other place to go. She was stuck. Alone at home with two small children Vicki went over and over what had happened. Hurt and hopelessness flooded over her. The contrast between the close relationships we had known for so long and this loneliness was more than she could bear. "I could find better friends in the world than here with God's people." She cried. "Why do we have to continue with discipleship? I'm ready to end our ties with everyone, especially the Lord."

Six weeks of constant anguish went by before a break came for her.

VICKI'S NEW VISION

One night I had a dream that left me very tired. I was unable to recall it the next morning. After a week I suddenly remembered the dream. I was lying in the middle of a stream of water floating very calmly along when suddenly I hit some rapids. As I was carried down the middle of the stream, I could see small streams off to the side, but could not get out of the center of the torrent. The rocks battered me and the force of the water tore my clothes away. Then, as suddenly as the rapids began, they stopped. I was once again in calm water. I was unable to move because of great pain, and I lay very still. I looked around and saw beautiful lily pads floating quietly toward me. The pads and their large colorful flowers began to cover my bruises and nakedness. The dream left me with a deep sense of peace.

For the first time in months, I sought God and his help in interpreting the dream. I felt that the Lord told me he was stripping away all that was unreal in my life in order to help me see what had been written on my heart. This did not excuse the treatment we had received, but it did help me begin again to have hope. God really was involved with us and that was enough.

Although the next months were hard, God gave us some fellowship with others in Jacksonville. We had some close friends in Georgia who came to see us often. We had been in the same small group together in Mobile and had had the same pastor. The total feeling of isolation was somewhat relieved. We sought God's guidance as best we could for what to do next.

BACK TO MOBILE

Through the next several months we talked with Gerrit and other friends in Mobile and decided that we would move back. My company in Jacksonville wanted to open a branch office in Mobile and it seemed tailor-made for me. They would pay our moving expenses and everything seemed to fall into place.

All the months of feeling out of place were coming to an end. This time things would be different! We had assurances that our relationship with Gerrit would now be permanent. We would no longer have to wonder if the relationship could end at any time. We were returning to old friends and some new ones, but the territory was familiar. We spiritualized the time and pain in Jacksonville by saying that it was God's will for conforming us into Christ's image. We returned to our eternal relationships. We had lost our idealism and had greatly lowered our expectations of ourselves, of our pastor, and of the Lord. But we were going home.

6

THE NEW COVENANT

INWARD FOCUS

The end of the 1970s changed the focus of the Mobile church. Much was now being said about reaching out. In the early 1980s the church began building a campus of buildings on forty acres of prime real estate as a means of developing an identity in Mobile. But as individuals many of us were actually turning inward. Although doctrinally we opposed the me-generation attitude prevalent during this period, many followers who had once centered their lives on evangelism and outreach now turned their attention toward jobs and families. Extensive teaching on excellence and the importance of doing well on the job had the expected result of producing many good workers.

The focus of *New Wine Magazine* shifted toward political, economic, and social issues of the day. The emphasis was on "getting it right before you share it." There were always many more people working on getting it right than there were sharing it. We were, in many ways, much more self- and much less Christ-centered in our thinking and actions.

LOWERED EXPECTATIONS

Myself

I decided that I was called to be a layman. The desire that I had had as a new Christian to preach and teach the Bible had lessened. There was so much else to do. This was, of course, not a lower call, but to me it meant giving up my dreams and any ideas of full-time ministry. I decided to pursue my career in sales and raise a Christian family. All the same, I felt that if only I could get my sales up and get out of debt, maybe God could use me someday. In the meantime, I would serve where I could in the church and forget the ministry as a full-time vocation. Financial success eluded me for several years although I did better than most. However, the gracious southern lifestyle that seemed so important to us was expensive and debts built slowly but surely. Savings or investments for the future were out of the question.

Pastor

Fellowship and closeness to a pastor was less important to us now. My pastor was much more interested in encouraging entrepreneurial ventures than he was in making disciples. Most of us had been related to him for years and he assumed that by that time we were pretty low-maintenance disciples. An hour or two of his time, interrupted by phone calls, once or twice a month was all that it meant to have a pastor. That was the extent of our fellowship. In any real spiritual sense the relationship ceased to function. But "appearances" were continued for six more years.

God

I could get excited about the great things God was doing with *New Wine Magazine* without ever being challenged to pray or read the Bible myself. I could go to church and participate in exuberant worship and yet not really expect God to do anything through me or for me or for those around me. I was spiritually numb, but I was busy and in a secure fellowship that made it easier to face my empty prayer life.

Not surprisingly, I had little interest in sharing my faith with others or inviting them to church. We were the spiritual marines and I could not find anyone I thought would be willing to pay the price I had paid for what I had.

THE SOUND TEAM

I became involved on the sound team because of its similarity to my background in television. At first, we had no building so at each meeting the equipment had to be set up from scratch in different locations. One Sunday each month we held our service downtown at the civic center. We found we could save a good deal of money with the professional sound contractor we used if we furnished all the manpower. That way we would only pay for the rental of his equipment and his personal time. The sound for our worship service was more complex than any of the big-name concerts he did. That meant that although we began set-up by six or six thirty in the morning, we would barely be ready for the nine thirty rehearsal. In spite of the sacrifice involved, serving and fulfilling a purpose in the church was a joy.

The Replacement

Rumor had it that I was about to be replaced as leader of the sound team. I asked my pastor, who was on the worship team, about it, and he replied, "Are *you* the leader of the sound team?" Pain and disappointment went through me like a knife when my pastor and friend for fifteen years said those words. I had been recognized by the church administrator as the leader—I thought everyone knew that. What had I done wrong? What could I have done better? It was too late. I felt exactly like I had been fired from a job I thought I had been doing fairly well at.

I was too "spiritual" to let anyone see that I was offended, but I was deeply hurt. Being part of the sound team was the only consistent thing I had "done for the Lord" in fifteen years as a Christian. And now even that had been taken from me. Within a few hours I realized that, in the eyes of the church leadership, I was forever identified with sound and television. As far as they were concerned, there was nothing else I could ever do. This loss was just a culmination of years of misunderstanding and rejection. I thought of leaving the church. Now there seemed to be no way to get from where I was to where I knew I needed to be. Just for an instant, I thought about suicide—about giving up on life itself, but the feeling left as quickly as it came.

THE WONDER OF WORSHIP

The Holy Spirit has a way of keeping us until his wind blows on us again. He began a process of removing me from the things that were hindering my walk with God. It began with the rediscovery of worship. Our church had always had rich, exuberant praise and worship, but the choruses now seemed to have more substance to them. They were becoming almost like hymns, yet the music was contemporary. Teaching on worship became more Bible centered. The church was supposed to be a kingdom of priests. All believers were part of this priesthood. We were to be priests in the home and on the job—continually offering sacrifices of praise.

This emphasis in Gerrit's teaching began to open old wells of love for God that had gotten plugged up over the years.

Experiencing the presence of God in regular, high worship gradually revealed my need for spiritual renewal. Five instances served to reawaken the call of God on my life to his service by breaking down my old thought patterns about God, the church, and myself. I was recovering the reason I had sought discipling in the first place.

THE PUBLIC MISTAKE

The first step toward renewal involved Charles Simpson himself. He has always displayed a remarkable and unique wisdom and professionalism in public, and I had never seen him make a mistake in judgment. But one night, in a congregational meeting, he publicly rebuked a man for asking a question that seemed to me, and many others, perfectly legitimate. He tried to smooth it over several times during the meeting, and later, apologized in a way that struck me as inappropriate. Years later those we interviewed still cited this incident as a turning point in their lives. Many realized for the first time that their admiration and respect for this man had become a form of dependence, even idolatry. As for myself, I had come to trust more on his being right than I trusted my own ability to hear God.

We all need to have our heroes brought down to size once in a while, or else we will worship them. Seeing him make what I thought was a very big, and very public mistake of judgment helped me to see that I could make mistakes too, and not be rejected by God for his service. It also helped me to see that Charles Simpson might have made other mistakes that I had not seen. God certainly had not rejected him for making them. Suddenly, "getting it all right" didn't seem to matter as much as getting "right" with God.

THE COVER IS OFF

"Covering," in the jargon of the shepherding movement, refers to the function of spiritual protection that a pastor has in the life of the believer. To come under submission to his authority was compared to coming in out of the rain. Ideally, this covering served to protect us from temptations and trials that we would have had to face alone. For many of us however, after a period of years, this covering became a lid. The purpose of discipleship was to equip followers to extend the ministry of their leader. If the ministry flourished, the leader needed us to help bear his load. But if his ministry languished, we were stuck.

The removal of my covering, and the second step of renewal, began when Gerrit Gustafson, one of Charles Simpson's first disciples,[1] and my pastor, stopped pastoring. He was not rejecting *us* this time. He was rejecting his job description as a pastor. He felt more comfortable as a teacher of principles of worship. He remained an elder in the church for some time, but conflicts developed that he apparently felt were matters of conscience. In time he was asked to resign and leave the church.

It was then that he apologized to me for some instances where he felt he had prevented me from doing the things God had called me to. I was lucky. Most pastors either never realized the problems they had created, or chose not to admit them. It was not Gerrit's apology that cleared the air for me though. It was nice, and it was a start, but what he had done was far beyond a mere "I'm sorry." In a way he, and the discipling movement, had interrupted the flow of my life for fifteen years. For more on this, see chapter 10.

REDISCOVERING THE FOUNDATIONS

Almost immediately after being released by him, I was asked by one of the leaders to teach a course on the basics of Christianity to the many new believers that were coming into his group. He said that the materials prepared by the church seemed to assume that the learner had some religious background. He needed something that began at the beginning, and gave me a free hand to do what I thought was best.

I thought of the foundation that had been laid in my life by my involvement with Campus Crusade for Christ. Rather than reinventing the wheel as our movement had always seemed to do in situations like these, I simply adapted from Campus Crusade literature several ideas from what had come to be known as the Transferrable Concepts. During the time I spent in preparation, the presence of God would seem to fill the room with light beyond what was coming in the windows.

I taught the class in six-week hour-and-a-half sessions. During these times of presenting simply and biblically our place in Christ through his finished work on the Cross, I realized his acceptance of us is unconditional. There is nothing we can do to make us more acceptable to God than what Jesus has already done for us on the Cross. I learned later I was in good company. Martin Luther arrived at much the same conclusion in very similar circumstances. After years of emphasis on community life, I was rediscovering my individual relationship with Jesus Christ.

I had been living my life on the basis that if I could just get out of debt, be more prosperous, have more obedient children, eat healthier food, and landscape my yard, I could qualify for some promotion to leadership and ministry. Like the Galatians, I believed that since God had been so good to me I had better get down to business if I want anything else from him.

The gospel of Christ's finished work on the Cross was the gospel I was called to proclaim, the gospel of the kingdom of God, not the gospel of government in the church. God assured us that before very long he was going to do a much better job of establishing his government on the earth than we could ever imagine. We were called, like Jesus, to "preach good news to the poor. . . . to proclaim freedom for the prisoners and recovery of sight for the blind, to release the oppressed, to proclaim the year of the Lord's favor" (Luke 4:18–19).

THE CALL TO MISSIONS

I was ready to go to the mission field to proclaim the good news. I was ready to pull down strongholds, uproot the kingdoms of darkness, and bring the gospel to the heathen. In that regard, I made three trips to the West Indies and was encouraged in fellowship by three local pastors who are the wisest, most resourceful, and most honest servants of God I have ever known. The need was there, the hearts were open, and I was ready. This call to missions was the fourth step toward spiritual renewal.

THE BIG ONE

Through Charles Simpson's mistake, my pastor's resignation, my renewed understanding of the Cross, and now a call to the nations, my love for God and my zeal for his word and work began to return. But as always, I probably would have done nothing more—until God had the last word.

The company I was working for began to experience a slowdown in sales and I decided to personally call on all my dealers in three months. I was already traveling in excess of 180 days a year and felt that this additional separation from my family would not be wise. We decided to travel together—all six of us. After over ninety days on the road we had had enough togetherness, but were drawn together in a very special way. As we traveled we visited shepherding-movement churches around the southeast. I found that the problems we had experienced in Mobile were more or less common to all the affiliated churches.

My sales effort, though, was not enough and in September, 1988 I was fired. The company closed its doors the following spring. What seemed like a setback at the time was actually the fifth step of renewal because we moved to Huntsville, Alabama, where we lived with my parents in order to help take care of my mother who had Alzheimer's disease. I also obtained a new job that required little out-of-town travel. Through this I gained valuable time in which to seek God for his direction.

NEW DIRECTIONS

While in the West Indies, I had been told of two institutions that had excellent reputations for producing missionaries, and that were sensitive to the culture to which the missionary was sent. One was Elim Bible Institute and the other was Asbury Theological Seminary. We visited both institutions, and began study at Asbury in September, 1989—exactly fifteen years after the discipleship adventure began.

At Asbury considerable spiritual and intellectual resources became available to help us discover what had happened and to reconstruct our lives. We were out of the movement but it was far from being out of us.

What is so sickeningly painful is that the good fruit in the lives of the people and the apparent soundness of these doctrines created in us a kind of compliance toward excesses and abuse. We believed that the doctrines taught us in the shepherding movement were biblical. Because we believed in the Bible, we were stuck with believing the doctrines long after the fruit went bad.

Was there something wrong with us for longing to belong to a church that had control over our private lives? We don't think the situation was that simple. We were not giving up our freedom—we thought we were becoming freer to follow Jesus.[2]

7

ALL THAT GLITTERS
IS NOT GOLD

THE GOSPEL OF DEATH

The Gospel brings new life to those who are spiritually dead. The shepherding movement has increasingly brought spiritual death to those who were once spiritually alive. Former followers are not really interested in following Jesus anymore, and former leaders want never to minister the Word again. Those who have managed to salvage a measure of their Christian life have difficulty relating in any church environment. Most cannot allow themselves to be vulnerable to anyone—being used and then being deeply hurt by those they trusted removes all hope that any relationship can be truly enjoyed. Worse yet, compliance, formed by trust in our leaders and their doctrines, appears to implicate us as willing participants in our own abuse.[1] I have often said, "No one put a gun to my head and made me stay. It was my own idea to go back to Mobile after being twice betrayed." But there is more to it than that.

What went wrong? How did those loving, serving, strong churches described in chapters 3 and 4 cause so much damage?

PREACHING OR PRACTICE

The present and former leadership maintains that the problem was not in what was taught, but in how the teaching was applied. Bob Mumford expressed the problem as one of orthodoxy versus orthopraxis—doctrine versus practice. The concepts were misapplied. The stories are numerous and all too familiar to us who were in the movement. Overzealous application of so-called spiritual authority has devastating aftereffects.

Does misapplication, though, explain the serious and lasting damage that has been done to so many lives? Our problems go far beyond misunderstanding and misapplication. *If misapplication were the only problem, then we would all have been guilty of being willing participants in our own abuse.* No, in some way we had to believe that what was being done to us was somehow *right*—that ultimately those in the leadership over us were only doing what the Scriptures taught and eventually things would work out for us. The doctrines we believed kept us from seeing the abuse that was happening right before our eyes.

To those of us in the movement, these ideas were different from what other churches and teachers were saying, but seemed much more biblical. Please remember, almost all of us came into the movement disenchanted with traditional denominational Christianity, and were willing to try new things.

We were not stupid. Michael Harper lists no fewer than five councils who found nothing outside "the bounds of allowable variety in the Body of Christ" with what was being taught in the movement.[2]

THE BEREAN PRINCIPLE

These councils were usually called to address some obvious instance of abuse that had come to their attention. Our leaders would agree that there had been abuse, apologize for it, and all would be forgiven. That is until the next time.[3]

Some members of these councils referred to their arguments as being appeals to the Berean principle—the supposed basis of what the Jews of Berea did in response to Paul's teaching. The council members usually trotted out a "proof text" verse or two to drive home their point. The problem is that so-called proof texts can be found to dismiss any doctrine as being unbiblical—even original sin or the Trinity. I never heard anything that seemed like abuse to me at the time, and dismissed their minor scriptural concerns with the feeling that we had plenty of verses that supported what we were doing.

Actually, the Bereans did not compile proof texts. In Acts 17:11, we find they "received the message with great eagerness and examined the Scriptures every day to see if what Paul said was true." They were not consulting the Scriptures as a lawyer would his law books in order to build a convincing argument. They were not trying to prove Paul and Barnabas wrong. They were simply checking to see if what was being taught was "in there."

It is with much embarrassment that I say that in fifteen years of involvement with the movement, I never once looked circumspectly at what we were doing to see if what we practiced was indeed in the Scriptures. Our teachers did that so thoroughly and convincingly that I never really thought about it. What we undeniably had was a collection of verses that seemed to fit what we believed about the early church. But many of our conclusions were made in the light of twentieth-century Western culture. Theologians call this type of biblical study "eisegesis." Eisegesis involves reading into a Scripture ideas that are not there or that were probably not intended by the writer, resulting in an interpretation that is not compatible with the context. This is a dangerous way to use the Scriptures.

This is not to say all the ideas in the shepherding movement were bad, but many were just not in the Bible, at least not in the same form in which they were taught to us. Put together, they represented a form of Christianity not found in the New Testament.

I never heard any secret, wildly heretical teaching. All of the concepts below were taught publicly by the leaders and are so footnoted. The applications given are how we as followers perceived and lived out what was taught. We received constant encouragement from our pastor and our friends that our understandings were correct.

In this chapter, and in the next two, we lay out the sources and some of the resulting abuses of the seven key principles of the movement. Also we offer for the first time, as far as we know, some of the problems with the Scriptural interpretations that are behind the doctrines.

AUTHORITY AND FELLOWSHIP

The most obvious example of eisegesis was in our understanding of authority. Derek Prince is quoted as saying, "Whenever his [God's] delegated authority touches our lives, he requires us to acknowledge and submit to it, just as we would to him in person."[4] We were to submit to leadership as if we were submitting to God.

In the June 1974 "New Wine Forum," Bob Mumford answered the question, "What is delegated authority and how do we recognize it and relate to it?"

> The fact that men neglect and abuse the authority they have been given is a foregone conclusion. This does not, however, give us excuse to withdraw from spiritual authority [that] which God has set in the church.[5]

This perverse emphasis on the importance of church authority simply because it is church authority has plagued and paralyzed the church since the time of St. Augustine. In all fairness, Bob Mumford did not make the statement to justify those who neglect and abuse. He wanted to stress the importance of obeying church authority even if some people abused it. Nevertheless, the damage was done, and obeying church authority became more important than protecting followers from the abuses of that authority. With our understanding of delegated authority, obedience to an abusive pastor was the same as obedience to God. After all, God knew what he was doing, everything would work together for good.

All of life's decisions were to be checked out with one's pastor, even the most personal ones. We enthusiastically gave our pastor the veto power over our plans, calling, and vocation, knowing he was committed to helping us find God's will for our lives. Decisions about major purchases and investments were always submitted to one's pastor. Homes and automobile models were suggested, and business plans were accepted, rejected, or revised on the advice of our pastor. All singles at any age were expected to ask the permission of their pastors before going on a date.

Apart from accepting Christ, marriage is the most important decision a believer can ever make. The individual's pastor was there to help make that decision the right one. Many singles appeared to be saved pain and heartbreak by committing this most important decision to their pastor. Much time and effort was saved when he said that he had someone in mind and promised to talk to the other individual's pastor about it. Someone on the outside was more objective, and better able to know who would make a good partner. An objective leader was also better able to know when a believer was mature enough for marriage. "Wise" couples put off marriage until their pastors agreed the time was right. The message was that couples who were willing to wait for their pastors' approval had a greater assurance that their marriage would be in the will of God. Pastors did not usually insist on obedience in the decision of marriage partners, however, pastors we knew did take a very active role in the process, providing input at every stage of the development of the relationship.

Pastors also helped decide how many children a couple should have and when they should have them. If the couple had no insurance or money for the medical bills, it was suggested that having children should be put off for a better time. Those with less earning potential were advised to limit their family size.

We believed that names have much greater spiritual significance than we normally put on them in Western culture. Some couples were "helped" by a careful pastor to choose the right name for a new baby. Adults often took the more formal use of their names or occasionally even took on an entirely new name at the suggestion of a pastor.

Pastors were concerned that their followers seek excellence in everything they did, and decorating the home was no exception.

One couple had chosen their furniture together, but when their pastor learned of their choices of color and style he was concerned that those choices did not reflect the best taste he felt they deserved and could afford. The husband and his pastor made the appropriate changes.

Loving correction administered by a pastor who was committed to the follower's welfare provided the means to obey when problems arose. Correction and rebuke were necessary if the pastor was going to have to "give an account" for a follower's actions. We sometimes called this correction "going through the fire." Like Daniel and his friends the object of correction was to go through the fire without smelling like smoke. This meant that we had to receive the rebuke without complaining—even when we thought he was wrong.

In the event that our pastor's advise seemed inappropriate, we could always have gone to his pastor. However, to have done so would have been not only a sure sign of my pastor's inability to lead me, but more importantly, a sign of my inability to follow. In either case, it could have meant being re-related to another pastor—and all the separation that that involved. I would have had to start all over with a new pastor; we would have had to begin again, forming new friendships after losing the friends we already had. It was just too high a price to pay. It seemed more spiritual to just trust and obey. Each time our wills and our pastor's will crossed it seemed like a chance for us to die to self, and bear our cross.

All of these actual testimonies of treatment are logical extensions of the teachings on spiritual authority contained in the statements made by Prince, Mumford, Simpson, and others. None of these examples could be considered direct misapplication of the quotations above or of other teaching by these men. As far as I can recall, there were no selfish motives at work in any of these examples—yet each of them resulted in profound emotional abuse.

If there is not something wrong with the teaching on delegated authority, why was there such damage? More on this in chapter 9.

Fellowship and authority always went hand in hand. Whenever a group got together, it seemed like someone always had to be in charge. The combination of so-called close interpersonal relationships and authoritarian leadership gave us a sense of identity that was determined by our place of fellowship. The first question asked of a new acquaintance in the church was, "Who is your pastor?"

We adapted a line from *Fiddler on the Roof*, "Because of our relationships, everyone of us knows who he is, and what God expects him to do." When they became difficult, "teaching" got us through.

Christian fellowship in the movement consisted mainly of the social interaction among those who were in committed relationships with the same pastor. Our relationships were important to us. The relationships gave the illusion of being close friendships since, in a way, we were already committed to each other by being committed to the same pastor. But these friendships were not the same as those that existed outside our system. In some ways, the shepherding movement's system of authority distorted the way we learned to make relationships. It fostered growth in some areas of relating and retarded it in others. The result was that when the authority system was removed, we found that large portions of the relationships between us and our friends were not real— a real shock to us. The normal process of give-and-take that is part of being a friend was denied us and was replaced with submission and authority.

Certainly authority was the root of the problem with the shepherding movement and it has been given its own chapter. The first of the branches from the root was our teaching and practice of sacrificial service to those who held that authority.

AS UNTO THE LORD—SERVING

The church of the New Testament was a church that served and gave to one another. The result was that "There were no needy persons among them" (Acts 4:34). Jesus' example of servanthood was revolutionary. The leader served his followers. No other religious figure in history had ever done that.

The types of service, both given and received, that

we described in chapters 3 and 4 were a powerful testimony to the world. Neighbors were impressed with the teams of workers who helped move church members into their new homes. Neighbors were touched by the outpouring of help and support that surrounded anyone in the church with a serious illness. But instead of remaining a witness to the world, serving gradually became a form of voluntary slavery—we called it being a bond servant—as described in Deuteronomy 15:16–17:

> But if your servant says to you, "I do not want to leave you," because he loves you and your family and is well off with you, then take an awl and push it through his ear lobe into the door, and he will become your servant for life.

Paul used this image of love and service when he called himself a servant of the church in Colossians 1:25. In the shepherding movement, this service to the church became an equally dedicated bondservice to the personal needs of those in leadership. What began in the Spirit became an occasion for the flesh. How did such a basic principle of the New Testament become so perverted and damaging?

The Reversal

The public teaching of the movement did clearly describe the New Testament model of serving in terms of Jesus' life of self-sacrificing service to his followers. But the roles reversed when it was understood that leaders served by leading—by leading, they were laying down their lives for their followers. Ideally, serving does not require reciprocity, but rather a sense of gratitude because this supposed great service will naturally lead the one who is sincere to look for ways to serve the one who is serving. This noble tendency was codified by Charles Simpson, "A disciple becomes a recipient of the favor and love given him, therefore he must be desirous of being a servant worthy of that favor."[6]

But in the context of the shepherding movement, it was the leader who loved and favored and the follower who served. The follower was a "recipient of the favor and love given him," and he "owed" service to the leader. The emphasis placed on the leader's authority, combined with a willingness on the part of the follower to be a servant, brought about a great reversal of Jesus' pattern of service. The result was the world's pattern of a follower's obedience to a leader's will. The follower had no recourse. To do anything else would be seen as a refusal to follow Christ's example of a suffering servant.

The Hook

Ern Baxter, in a wonderful balanced article on Jesus' example of serving his disciples, states:

> There is probably no Christian reading this article who has not known the supreme and inexpressible joy of having served another out of sheer love for Christ, and for the one being served. It is like nothing else that one has ever known. Should there ever be a hint of resentment, or the least suggestion in our spirit that we are being taken advantage of, our Lord reminds us that we must take another look at Him who "did not come to be served, but to serve, and to give his life a ransom for many." He becomes the supreme example of a love slave. Until we have gone as far as He has gone in submission to the demands of love, we cannot hold a resentment or bear a grudge, or refuse to gird ourselves with a towel and wash the feet of a brother who has picked up the contamination of the road of life.[7]

The context reveals that there was a noble sentiment in these statements. But when this understanding was combined with our hierarchical relationships, the many obvious instances of being taken advantage of had to be ignored by the follower, and regarded as the inability to see Jesus as his or her example. The result in many groups was a particularly cruel form of psychological slavery.

Men, who worked regular hours at their own jobs, were expected to volunteer time to help salaried workers build and maintain leaders' houses. Such work took every evening away from their families for months. One of these houses was over three thousand square feet and had four bedrooms. During the short time the owner/leader occupied the house he and his wife had no children. Many leaders reaped enormous equity from houses built or remodeled in this way.

A church was raising money to build a new building. One of the pastors of the church, in order to earn the money he had committed would come from his small group, contracted with a local hotel to repair and renew all its bathrooms. As good servants, the men of his group were expected to help, but this "good cause" required that they work every week night and every Saturday for months.

One man gave up a successful construction business in the Midwest to move to Mobile. He was unable to find a job, and between interviews worked full-time without pay on the new church building, supporting himself with his savings. Finally he found a job in another city. His contribution as a professional contractor was very significant, but because he took a job before the buildings were completed, he was forgotten and his contribution was never recognized. He hadn't done it for recognition, though, and he left in generally good spirits considering that he was at least $10,000 poorer.

The men were not the only ones who served. Married women often spent considerable time helping leaders' wives, often leaving them little time to keep their own homes. This put them in a double bind, since the condition of their own home was considered a reflection on their husband's ability to lead. Single women often found every spare hour filled with free babysitting and housekeeping chores. Frequently this meant that they missed church meetings or social events so a married couple could attend.

Looking back, I recall an instance where we briefly had a single woman living in our home after the birth of our first child. The four of us had all returned from a meeting at midnight to the dinner dishes still in the sink. It was automatically assumed that Millie would wash the dishes before going to bed. She sang softly and joyfully as she worked, but the only way I could prevent Vicki from helping her was by telling her that Millie needed to learn to serve, and we could best help her by letting her go on alone. Fortunately for her, she was with us only a few weeks. Such preposterous treatment is beyond a mere "I'm sorry." Millie, if you read this, please understand I was selfish and I now understand some of its effect on you.

Even though this type of service was widespread, there were some who were not taken in by it. Those who were children at the time saw through the religious whitewash to the plain human selfishness. They are now in their late teens and early twenties and some have told us in effect, "If this is what serving God is like, I want no part of him." A few of the leaders had the integrity to see the problem and refused to allow their followers to mow their lawns or wash their cars. They were the exception rather than the rule and were unusually viewed as not giving their followers opportunity to learn to serve.

But Jesus said,

> For I was hungry and you gave me something to eat, I was thirsty and you gave me something to drink, I was a stranger and you invited me in, I needed clothes and you clothed me, I was sick and you looked after me, I was in prison and you came to visit me. Then the righteous will

answer him, "Lord, when did we see you hungry and feed
you, or thirsty and give you something to drink? When did
we see you a stranger and invite you in, or needing clothes
and clothe you? When did we see you sick or in prison and
go to visit you?" The King will reply, "I tell you the truth,
whatever you did for one of the least of these brothers of
mine, you did for me" (Matt. 25:35–40).

Jesus service was directed downward. While it is true that
Jesus came to do the Father's will, his service was directed
to us. He humbled himself. He washed his disciple's feet.
He literally laid down his life on our behalf. Now he
forever makes intercession before the Father on our
behalf. In this passage in Matthew Jesus asks from us the
same kind of downward directed service, and then
personally identifies with those we are to serve, calling
them his brothers.

Our system—serving those in leadership—was a
perversion of Christ's example. We were not learning to
serve as Jesus did—we were being exploited by our
leaders for their own personal gain. Little we did had
anything to do with learning to serve the Lord. God may
yet use those experiences for good in our lives and in the
lives of others, but we must understand that that form of
serving was not God's will. This must be understood by
everyone if the suffering that we followers feel is to be
relieved.

Not only did Christ's example become perverted, so
did we. I enjoyed the status that went with the opportunity to wash Charles Simpson's classic Oldsmobile con-
vertible. It seemed more significant than helping a family
we hardly knew move. For me there was a kind of
perverted pride that went with serving someone in
leadership. I have to confess that as sin.

But confession is not all there is. We can no longer
hide behind statements like: "Nobody put a gun to my
head and made me serve like that," or "What an idiot I

was to let myself be taken in like that." We were set up. We were not only abused by a selfish pastor, but the false teaching, perpetrated in the name of serving, desensitized us to what was actually happening. We trusted our pastor, and we were betrayed.

COVENANT LOYALTY

The Middle Eastern custom of establishing covenant loyalty through having a meal together, "passing salt," was the basis for the high place given to loyalty in the shepherding movement. In his *New Wine* article on loyalty, Charles Simpson distinguished between loyalty to truth and loyalty to people, concluding that God wants us to be loyal to people. Following a humorous description of his former fundamentalist penchant for verbal combat with heretics, he says:

> It dawned on me, God's covenant is not with doctrines, as important as they may be; God's covenant is with people. God's faithfulness is to people. Jesus died for people.
>
> Men do not exist to serve truths. Truths exist to serve men. "The Sabbath was made for man, not man for the Sabbath" (Mark 2:27).[8]

In this article, he also quoted Mark 9:50. "Salt is good, but if it loses its saltiness, how can you make it salty again? Have salt in yourselves, and be at peace with each other." To lose saltiness is to lose loyalty. In contrast to sand, salt naturally sticks to itself. Thus, "to have salt in yourselves" means to be loyal to one another. If a follower is not loyal he or she is useless. Simpson presented this verse as being Jesus' teaching on loyalty.

However, the context, beginning with verse 42, is referring to sin, not loyalty. It is improbable that Jesus was specifically referring to the disciples' loyalty to one another or their loyalty to him in this passage. Instead, it is more probable that he was referring to their mutual loyalty to the covenant relationship, which he has just described as that which takes all possible precautions against sin. It is the preserving nature of salt, not its cohesiveness, that is the emphasis of the salt analogy in the Gospels.

This misuse of the Scripture confused and artificially separated the issues of sin and loyalty. Loyalty to people became the standard for relationships. Loyalty took precedence over concern for their victory over sin. Loyalty overlooked sin and as a result an individual's sin could be treated lightly for many years—as long as that person was loyal. Jesus' taught that Christians should be loyal to one another, and that loyalty is to be manifested by encouraging one another to victory over sin. We, however, hid sin under the covering of loyalty.

A young man of our congregation overheard a conversation that was very uncomplimentary about another male member of the church. This man under discussion was a powerful, and apparently successful, farmer and produce processor, who had attained his position in our small valley by stepping on many toes. While what was said was essentially true, yet because the man was a prominent member of the church, the young man defended him vehemently, almost to the point of losing his job. The young man felt that covenant loyalty demanded a rigorous defense—in essence, the truth of the man's behavior had to be laid aside in order for the defense to be made.

The problem with this unholy separation between loyalty to truth and loyalty to people is that there becomes no way to separate rejection of false doctrine, or sinful, unwise behavior from rejection of the person. From our point of view, to confront a fellow follower or expose his or her sin was to be disloyal. That was the pastor's job. From a leader's point of view, every voice of disagreement became a personal attack and as such constituted disloyalty.

Each of us was often forced to make choices between our loyalty to each other and to truth. Each of us was taught to choose, in effect, to believe the lie that our personal relationships were more important than was freedom from sin. This ambivalence about truth and sin caused enormous emotional damage. It set us up to accept abuse from those in authority. It completely eliminated critical upward communication. The best kind of loyalty was blind. Every time we went along with this teaching, it was as if another piece of our souls died. The same ambivalence now seriously impairs our ability to enjoy any relationship or accept anything as truth, even the Gospel.

KINGDOM TAXES

Anyone who has been reached by the grace of God knows that as a believer there is a desire to give. That desire was present in our lives as well, and we tithed. However, for many years the amount we tithed roughly equaled our consumer indebtedness. This was particularly embarrassing because we had bought in to the "health-and-wealth gospel" that boldly claims Luke 6:38, "Give, and it will be given to you. . .pressed down, shaken together and running over," as its doctrinal basis. The only thing we had that was running over when we tithed was red ink. If I needed more money, I felt I should give more. For me, tithing was my greed dressed in its Sunday best.

Of course, the shepherding movement did not have a monopoly on this perversion of Christianity. Ministries abound that promise their listeners "the riches of the kingdom" if they will only send in their pledges. Testimonies circulated in our group of how tithing had led to dramatic increases in salary. These so-called financial success stories made one want to tithe, if only to get in on the action. Good news preached to the poor became the good news that would make us rich. This twisted understanding of the Word has, at least partially, been exposed for the lie that it is. The secular media has seen through the blue smoke and mirrors to the greed and sin that was at the bottom of this thinking, but spiritually gifted saints remained blind to it.

Houses and Lands

Pastors theoretically were supposed to have a salary that was an average of that of their followers, and most pastors had about ten families under their care. If ten families were to give ten percent of their income, then mathematically it would work out that the pastor would receive the same income as his followers. We soon noticed, however, that this was not the case. Pastors normally had much nicer houses and cars than did their followers. If anyone dared question this inequity, he or she was told that the spiritual (correct) action was for them to be grateful that God's faithful servants were being rewarded. I knew that since I was following Jesus, I would have all that myself someday.

The Amateur Factor

What was actually happening was, that as a pastor's group grew, he would re-relate some of his men to one of his other followers. This was viewed as a promotion for the new part-time pastor, though these "amateurs" were most often unpaid, since they usually had fewer than five in their group. This practice gave a paid pastor indirect authority over many more than just ten men. Thus, the tithes credited to him were greatly increased while his workload increased only slightly. The paid pastors worked to keep the organization structured in this way— obviously, if one of the amateurs became a full-time pastor, the paid pastor stood to lose all the tithes involved, since the new pastor would now have his own account. At its peak the church in Mobile had over 350 families, or about twelve hundred people in committed relationships. At the same time only twenty, or so, full-time pastors were on salary.

This "sales manager's dream" came to an end when the church began constructing buildings and the adding the obligatory staff. Increased assessments to the pastors' accounts coupled with shrinking membership required them to expand the practice of re-relating just to keep the bills paid. Eventually, paid pastors who weren't carrying their weight felt led to resign.

In such a system, economic support existed only for pastors. We were a church that believed in all the spiritual gifts and ministries (Rom. 12, 1 Cor. 12, and Eph. 4), but only those who had the gift of pastoring could receive a living from ministering the Word. Because we believed the tithe was the pastor's, other forms of ministry had no formal means of support, and, despite what we said we believed, we became a one-gift church. Those who were gifted as teachers or evangelists were free to start a traveling ministry or plant a church, but "seed money" to get started was never available. There was no way other forms of ministry could be self-sustaining. Unless a ministry or outreach could be presented as being self sustaining, it was considered by the leadership to be irresponsible. Over fifteen years we learned something about diligence and responsibility. Good qualities, but diligence is not dependence. At some point in the work of God there is always a time where we can do nothing but trust. That step was denied us.

To be in full-time ministry was to be in church

government, a very elite status that was the result of a promotion. But, because we were taught that "promotion is of the Lord," there was then no systematic path to ordination. The aspiration to the ministry as a vocation was considered pretentious since a measure of church political power supposedly went with it. There were, however, those who had been trained, gained experience, or were ordained *elsewhere* who achieved positions of leadership in shepherding churches. We do not remember even one disciple who came to Christ in the movement, received all his foundation and preparation from a pastor, and was subsequently promoted to a position of full-time vocational ministry. Our experience involves four churches over a fifteen-year period. We have been assured by others that this lack of promotion from within was widespread. Another even more malignant problem with the system involved the tithe and the personal pastor.

The Commissioned Pastor

One burned-out, slightly cynical former pastor, who had once been a salesman and who resigned as a pastor long ago, confessed to me that, try as he would, he could not help but view each family he pastored as being an economic unit of his income. This view affected his counseling. When one of his followers was seeking God's will to move to another city for a job promotion and to relate to another pastor, this pastor had a difficult time believing the impending move to be the will of the Lord— knowing his tithe would go with him. Giving his blessing would have had a very negative impact on his finances.

In reality, our pastors were paid on commission—the more tithes they brought in, the higher their salary. One former pastor told me had received over $100,000 one year in tithes from the ten or so families related to him.

There is no accounting of what other abuses resulted from this unholy combination of authoritarian leadership and the tithe.

FIRST THE NATURAL, THEN THE SPIRITUAL

Our brand of the now infamous health-and-wealth gospel naturally involved authority. Since the time of Constantine, the church has wrestled with the implications of the gospel in earthly matters. In the Old Testament it seems clear enough that God's will was done on earth by earthly kings. We know that a time will come when the saints will judge the world and the angels, and in some sense will rule with Christ from his throne. But do we share in his rule over earthly matters right now?

Charles Simpson used Scripture passages to teach that if we are going to rule when Christ returns, we had better learn how to do it by learning to rule over a few things now, a kind of on-the-job training. But, is this a conclusion implied by the passage, or imposed on it from another perspective?

In 1 Corinthians 6:1-3 we read:

> If any of you has a dispute with another, dare he take it before the ungodly for judgment instead of before the saints? Do you not know that the saints will judge the world? And if you are to judge the world, are you not competent to judge trivial cases? Do you not know that we will judge angels? How much more the things of this life!

Charles Simpson restated it this way: "It is important that you learn to settle the affairs of this life because you have been called of God to judge the world and even to judge angels! God has chosen us to reign over the affairs of His creation."[9]

Is this what Paul actually intended? Or was he appealing to a future reality in order to convince Christians to conduct themselves properly toward one another in the present? Is the issue here our loving conduct toward each other or our rule over each other? It was clear enough to us at the time that we could only learn to rule over "the affairs of His creation" by ruling over others in the church. The nature of this rule was "clear" in Revelation 2:26–29:

> To him who overcomes and does my will to the end, I will give authority over the nations—
>
> > He will rule them with an iron scepter;
> > He will dash them to pieces like pottery—
>
> just as I have received authority from my Father. I will also give him the morning star. He who has an ear, let him hear what the Spirit says to the churches.

Charles Simpson said:

> I believe God intends for every Christian to be an overcomer and to share in a measure in the reigning process. Revelation 3:21 says, "He who overcomes I will grant to him to sit down with Me on My throne, as I also overcame and sat down with my Father on His throne." In other words, overcomers will share in the reign and authority of God.[10]

The nature of our rule with Christ seemed obvious to us. The "reign and authority of God" that we share in was to "rule with an iron scepter." The numerous abusive applications of authority were partially the result of confusion about our present conduct toward one another and our future reign with Christ over creation.

> Now, I am not here to teach on eschatology or the end time. There is much that I don't understand about that subject. But whenever and however Jesus is coming, and whatever He is going to do, I cannot see the Lord giving the rule of all creation to a group of people who have not learned to tend to their own business. I believe if we are going to rule the world, we must first learn to rule our own spirit, our own soul, our own body, our own family, in the church, and then He will give us the earth to rule.[11]

Charles Simpson said he was not teaching on the end time, but all the scriptures he used are encouragements and exhortations that look toward the end time. No indication whatever is given in any of the Scripture passages of any training process. This is not to say we should not rule our own spirit, our own soul, or our own body, but when he added, "our own family" and "in the church," to this context of supposed training for future rule, he introduced all the future implications into our present relationships.

The door was now open for leaders to exercise Jesus' authority over the personal earthly affairs of their followers. Furthermore, an issue that had divided the church for seventeen centuries, dominion of the church over secular affairs, was resolved for all time by looking at a few Scripture verses. We boldly rushed in "where angels fear to tread" and built a movement on a principle that was far from being a settled issue.

The "reigning process" was never confused with our building the kingdom of God in the sense of our bringing about Christ's return. But this teaching twisted the concept of our ruling with Christ at his coming into the understanding that we ought to rule with him over creation, the natural realm, and the church right now.

Relation of Natural and Spiritual

The purpose of our learning to rule in the natural realm was not only to learn how to reign over creation with Jesus, but also to learn to rule in spiritual matters. We were taught the "spiritual principle" of "first the natural then the spiritual."

> If there is a natural body, there is also a spiritual body. So it is written: "The first Adam became a living being"; the last Adam, a life-giving spirit. The spiritual did not come first, but the natural, and after that the spiritual. The first man

was of the dust of the earth, the second man from heaven. As was the earthly man, so are those who are of the earth; and as is the man from heaven, so also are those who are of heaven. And just as we have borne the likeness of the earthly man, so shall we bear the likeness of the man from heaven" (1 Cor. 15:44–49).

Charles Simpson comments:

I don't want to labor the resurrection, but I want to point out a principle here. Verse 46 says, "However, the spiritual is not first, but the natural: then the spiritual." I believe God deliberately chooses to teach man through the natural before He brings him to the spiritual. The natural is not unimportant. It is grade one before you go to grade two.[12]

This passage, however, is about resurrection—not faithfulness in natural things. Simpson has forced a meaning on this Scripture that is not there. The section beginning in 1 Corinthians 15:1, is addressing the chronology of natural and spiritual only in the context of the Resurrection. Its emphasis is just the opposite, the preeminence of the spiritual over the natural. The concern conveyed throughout the article quoted here is that good behavior in Christians is important. Simpson's concern was valid, but the reversal of the meaning of this Scripture also reversed our concept of the Christian life when this understanding of "first the natural" was combined with the health-and-wealth gospel prevalent in our church.

Principles of Natural Things

In the same article that was quoted above, Charles Simpson says that there are three principles Jesus was teaching in the parable of the shrewd manager as found in Luke 16:1-13.

So these are the three principles that have to do with natural things: (1) Faithful in a little, given much; (2) Faithful in money, given spiritual riches; (3) Faithful in another's, given that which is your own.[13]

Here is the parable:

There was a rich man whose manager was accused of wasting his possessions. So he called him in and asked him, "What is this I hear about you? Give an account of your management, because you cannot be manager any longer."

The manager said to himself, "What shall I do now? My master is taking away my job. I'm not strong enough to dig, and I'm ashamed to beg—I know what I'll do so that, when I lose my job here, people will welcome me into their houses."

So he called in each one of his master's debtors. He asked the first, "How much do you owe my master?"

"Eight hundred gallons of olive oil," he replied.

The manager told him, "Take your bill, sit down quickly, and make it four hundred."

Then he asked the second, "And how much do you owe?"

"A thousand bushels of wheat," he replied.

He told him, "Take your bill and make it eight hundred."

The master commended the dishonest manager because he acted shrewdly. For the people of this world are more shrewd in dealing with their own kind than are the people of the light. I tell you, use worldly wealth to gain friends for yourselves, so that when it is gone, you will be welcomed into eternal dwellings.

Whoever can be trusted with very little can be trusted with much, and whoever is dishonest with very little will also be dishonest with much. So if you have not been trustworthy in handling worldly wealth, who will trust you with true riches? And if you have not been trustworthy with someone else's property, who will give you property of your own?

No servant can serve two masters, Either he will hate the one and love the other, or he will be devoted to one and despise the other. You cannot serve both God and Money.

This is not an easy passage to interpret, but all indications are that the point Jesus was making was about the Pharisees' love of money. Why else would the Pharisees, who the Scripture says loved money, (natural things) sneer at Jesus? They were upset because Jesus was explaining his low regard for worldly resources. He was not teaching on faithfulness in natural things but, just the opposite—the overwhelming importance of spiritual things. In the last part of Luke 16:15 Jesus says, "What is highly valued among men is detestable in God's sight." Once again, Jesus' lesson on the preeminence of the spiritual had been twisted to make a point about faithfulness with natural things.

In the *New Wine* article quoted above, Charles Simpson gives several innocent-sounding examples to illustrate the three principles he had extrapolated from the parable in Luke 16. No one at the time disagreed with the examples, but his application of them as general principles resulted in great distortion.

"Faithful in a little, given much" meant that the measure of faithfulness in the little was the "much" that resulted. Great results meant great faithfulness. Poor results meant faithlessness. If you received a raise, it was because you were faithful. If your sales were off, God was having to withhold his blessing of much because of your unfaithfulness with a little. Financial success became the measure of faithfulness and diligence in the natural. Since the natural and the spiritual were seen as connected, we felt financial success or increase was one clear indication of spiritual maturity and God's approval.

"Faithful in money, given spiritual riches" meant that if one ever wanted to be considered as being spiritual, he must first be able to earn enough money, and manage it carefully enough to afford an upper-middle-class suburban-American lifestyle. Then God, seeing your faithfulness in natural things, would give you his spiritual blessings.

Proving oneself in the natural was what opened the doors to leadership positions within the shepherding movement. We believed that the people who were successful and had money would be the ones selected to lead, since they had proven themselves, and God had blessed them. The only path to full-time spiritual ministry was through some natural achievement.

A man, who obviously managed his finances well, moved to Mobile from another state. He became an administrator in our church, and was asked to write articles regarding money matters in church publications. When our group divided, he was given co-leadership of a group. This sequence of events made it transparent to us that his ability to manage his personal financial affairs led to his promotion to leadership.

Another man in our church, a seminary graduate and gifted speaker and debater, worked in a succession of jobs for over ten years. Although he managed to provide for his family, he never quite reached a level of financial success that was able to convince the leadership that he had God's approval. When he was given opportunity to minister to the youth, attendance dropped, and he was replaced. To our way of thinking, his lack of productivity in spiritual things was the result of his lack of fruitfulness in the natural.

We knew a couple who never seemed to have enough for a nice place to live or for nice clothes, but they always testified to how good God was to them spiritually. Their spiritual blessings were always suspect to most of us since they didn't appear to be faithful in money matters. Eventually they left the church and became missionaries to a poor area of a European country. Their ministry soon spread to Eastern Europe. We then realized that what we saw as their lack of faithfulness in natural things did not indicate a lack of ability or usefulness in spiritual things. In fact, the lack of material prosperity may well have prepared them for what lay ahead.

"Faithful in another's, given that which is your own" meant having a willingness to mow a leader's grass and wash his car if one ever wanted to have a house and lawn and a new car that nice of one's own. Taken one step further, we believed that if we served a leader who had a great ministry, God would see our faithfulness and give us a great ministry too.

Certainly God intends for our conduct, both material and spiritual, to be above reproach, but forcing concepts onto these Scriptures separates the natural from the spiritual. The Bible does not recognize this division. The result was an unholy concern with natural things to the neglect of a truly balanced life.

One of the leaders was returning from a trip with his family, and preparations were made to welcome them home. A friend of ours was asked to provide fruit for their homecoming. He thought he had been chosen because of his ability to select fruit, so he and his wife made a search of the local farmer's market and carefully selected the best of the best. Our friend's pastor, one of the leader's "men," was horrified to learn that the fruit had simply been delivered to the home in the box it had come in. He had expected our friend to simply call a caterer and have them deliver a prepared basket of fruit wrapped in green plastic. He was so incensed, he felt it necessary to buy one himself and give it to our friends. After all, they needed to know the "right" way to prepare a gift of fruit.

The fact that the fruit was probably the best available in the city was overlooked because of some missing green plastic. The obsession for excellence in the natural led to an inordinate concern for appearances. With this emphasis, style became more important than substance—in fruit and in life.

I was so preoccupied with the natural that I often found that I could not remember the name of someone I had just met at church, but I could recall details of his occupation. What they did for a living and how well they did it, was more important to me than who they were or what their needs might be. First the natural, then the spiritual was not what Jesus taught. It was simply the twentieth-century American work/success ethic. It is as alien to Christianity as Mother Teresa is to Donald Trump. First the natural, then the spiritual really meant first success, then power. The point was clear in *New Wine Magazine*:

> Those who gain mastery in their vocation make a place for themselves by virtue of their expertise. James B. Conant puts it this way, "Each honest calling, each walk of life, has its own elite, its own aristocracy based upon excellence of performance." It is essentially true that success will bring us to positions of authority and leadership.[14]

Jesus has already addressed the issue of our relationship to natural things in Luke 12:22–34. Verse 34 says: "For where your treasure is, there your heart will be also." Our preoccupation with natural things led us to a fascination with productivity.

The Myth of Maturity

The natural-then-spiritual idea did not originate with the shepherding movement. The Galatians also thought they had to be faithful in natural things after they became Christians.

> Are you so foolish? After beginning with the Spirit, are you now trying to attain your goal by human effort? Have you suffered so much for nothing—if it really was for nothing? Does God give you his Spirit and work miracles among you because you observe the law, or because you believe what you heard? [i.e., the gospel] Consider Abraham: "He

believed God, and it was credited to him as righteousness."
Understand, then, that those who believe are children of
Abraham. The Scripture foresaw that God would justify the
Gentiles by faith, and announced the gospel in advance to
Abraham. . . . (Gal. 3:3–8)

Abraham became the father of the "faithful," not by
diligence and good management of his resources but by
his faith in God. He believed God and was thus made
righteous before God prior to his having any natural
things with which to be faithful. For Abraham as well as
the Galatians, it was first the spiritual, then the natural!

One woman we were acquainted with had great
spiritual need, but often did not ask for prayer because
she was afraid it would make her and her husband appear
immature and unspiritual.

In the shepherding movement, spiritual maturity was
intertwined with productivity. The objective for a mature
Christian was to produce more than one consumed. The
trouble was, spiritually, we were all conspicuous con-
sumers. We felt we had some of the best Bible teaching,
pastoring, musicians, and worship in the body of Christ.
At the same time, however, we followers were not
recognized as ones who should produce anything spiritual.

The result was that I feigned spiritual maturity by
becoming a low-maintenance disciple. By reducing to an
absolute minimum the spiritual resources I consumed,
such as my pastor's time, I gave the impression that I was
stable and mature. Vicki and I were actually in great need,
but to admit to that need would have required us to
consume too many resources.

In recent years, I have discovered that the farther I go
in my walk with God, the more I need his resources. I
find I will never come close to producing more spiritual
resources than I have consumed in receiving Jesus'

sacrifice on the Cross. I now thank God I don't have to, for Jesus produced them for me.

UNRAVELING

We built fifteen years of our lives on the pillars of authority, service, loyalty, tithing, and natural things. These false and syncretistic ideas have exacted a heavy toll on us. The damage done by the shepherding movement originated in what our leaders taught—not just in wrong application. It's time to let the Scriptures speak.

Someone has counted all the verses in the Bible. If their count is correct (we didn't check), the middle verse is Psalms 118:8: "It is better to take refuge in the Lord than to trust in man." But over the fifteen years we were involved, the church and its pillars gradually became the focus of our lives. We expected our interpersonal relationships and obedience to the teaching we received to provide what we needed. We were learning diligence, not dependence—especially not dependence on Christ. Eventually we turned more to men and the system they had developed than to the redeeming work Jesus Christ had accomplished on the Cross.

The pillars have become a net of wrong ideas that separates those who followed a shepherd from much of the grace of God. But, the most dangerous part of the net was the order of the home and its relationship to the government of the church.

8

"GOD'S" ORDER
IN THE HOME

VICKI'S STORY

Ron's company had decided to close his sales territory, and in ten days he would be out of a job. We were sitting in his office at home discussing what God would have us do next when he received a call; a woman who had left the church with much hurt and bitterness needed encouragement. As she and Ron talked, my mind wandered and I was startled to hear an almost audible voice say to me, "your deliverance was for you." The year before, I had received extensive ministry and counseling from friends while Ron had been away on business. He had been overjoyed at what God had done for me, and I had been glad the Lord had freed me to make me a better helpmate, better able to serve Ron.

It took a few moments for me to realize that that voice was the Lord's and he was saying something life-changing to me—*Your deliverance was for you!!!* It was not to further Ron's walk with Lord, it was not to bless him, it was not for any other reason except that Jesus loved me and wanted me to be free. The more I thought about those words, the more excited I became. As Ron's conversation with our friend continued I began to see how blind I had been. Feelings of liberty and love in Christ began to wash over me. I couldn't believe how free I felt.

When Ron hung up, I excitedly blurted out to him what I had heard and was feeling. He was shaken. His voice was barely above a whisper as he said to me, "You didn't know that?" I thought he was going to weep. He was stunned by the realization of how much of my life had been lived for him. I thought everything God did for me was for him—to help him find his place in the kingdom, and pursue what God had called him to do.

Words cannot express what happened to us over the next several hours. Neither of us could believe how distorted our relationship had become. How could a relationship, ordained and blessed by God from the beginning with love and respect, have gotten so out of balance? I had somehow relinquished my place before God for Ron. In seeking to honor and make Ron the head of our home, I had also made him the lord of my life. I had even given him a Bible when we were first married and had signed it "to my lord" (with a small "l"), referring to Sarah's having called Abraham lord.

Ron seemed humiliated that this had ever happened to our relationship. He had never known the extent to which I was living my life through him. As you can imagine, he spent a lot of time before God the next few days repenting for what had happened. As for me, *I was free!!!*—Free to be me before the throne. . .free to stand by Ron's side as an heir to the kingdom. I had rediscovered my first love, my one and only Lord!

I took a long walk that afternoon and my world had somehow changed. Spiritual songs to my Father welled up and overflowed from my heart. I experienced a love feast with my Father. I was his creation and he had called me to be his child. He was working in my life to help *me*, to teach *me* his ways, to use *me*. I had lived my life through my husband and the church leadership to the neglect of most of my own personal relationship with Jesus.

A part of my life had come to an end, but *oh what a beginning*.

THE HOME A HIERARCHY

How did this happen? How did we wind up like this?

We understood that our home was a hierarchy. I was the head and was expected to love Vicki as Christ loved the church. She was the body and was to honor and submit to me in the same way she would submit to the Lord. We brought this model into our marriage. But, since I am not the Lord, the constant submission of her will to mine caused her to identify more with me and less with God. She felt that being my helpmate meant that her only purpose in life was to help me do what God had called me to do. It wasn't until 1988, after 14 years in the discipleship movement, that Vicki saw herself before God as his disciple.

In the discipleship/shepherding movement, wives were to submit and husbands were to love. Paul's familiar words in Ephesians 5:22 and 25 are followed by the statement in verse 32 that all of this is a great mystery. It was our understanding that two thousand years of church history had added little to our understanding of the mystery. The less sincere husbands among us were content to leave it at being a mystery, but it seemed clear to everyone else exactly what "wives be in subjection to your own husbands" meant—wives, fit into your husband's plans.

A wife's submission to her husband was a fairly easy thing to evaluate. The mystery of how a husband was to love his wife was another matter, and he was free to interpret it in his own way (not that there was a lack of teaching on the matter). At least part of that interpretation meant that a husband was responsible to spiritually "wash" his wife from the cares of the world and from the duties of home. He was also expected to be her counselor and help her apply biblical principles and teaching to her problems. Flowers, gifts, and dinners out each weekend were given to make her feel special. In essence, he was personally responsible for her happiness by being all she needed. Thus, the job of husband gradually became that of being his wife's personal savior in all temporal matters.

Vicki never had to seek God for direction because it was my responsibility to hear God and lead the family. If she actually received direction from God, she had to check it out with me first. If I didn't agree, she knew to let it drop. Fasting or praying for herself became unnecessary—I was there and she was supposed to trust the revelation I received from God. If she did fast or pray, it was for God's guidance for me. I felt I was loving her "as Christ loved the church" by mediating her spiritual life, and by telling her what she should do. She was the keeper of the home, but she had no say over where, why, or what she kept. Everything revolved around what I desired. Of course, my desires were shaped by the expectations of my pastor. Vicki's desires were shaped by me and often by my pastor's wife.

Wives never had to face direct conflict with others inside or outside the church. Once, Vicki offered the use of our washer and dryer to a family who did not have their own. This was not the first time Vicki had ever made this offer, but this time there was a problem. The other woman began making almost daily visits, which often lasted several hours. The woman was a friend, and not wanting to offend, Vicki shared the problem with my pastor's wife. Apparently, my pastor told the woman's husband because it was not long before the problem no longer existed. No direct confrontation on Vicki's part had been necessary—she had not had to deal with the issue alone.

I lovingly encouraged Vicki to lose weight after each child. I reminded her that it was her job to empty all pockets before she washed my clothes. I firmly reminded her that she should always know what each church leader took in his coffee without having to ask. Out of loving concern for her safety, I told her she was to be home from errands and shopping before dark.

Actually, some things about being a husband in our church were quite simple. One piece of advice for couples was: "There is no need for Christian couples to have arguments. The husband should always have the last word, and the wife should always submit to it." Therefore, a wife never questioned her husband, since God had placed him "over" her. She never "uncovered" him by telling anyone about his problems. That would be usurping his authority as husband (his pastor was responsible to God for him, not her), and that was not her place as a wife. She was to submit to him, and through her submission, God would take care of her. This got her out of the way so that God could deal with her husband's shortcomings. As God, working directly and through her husband's pastor, made the necessary changes, her husband would then be better able to love her "as Christ loved the church."

Impossible Job

We men felt that we should be imitating the leadership in all things, including loving our wives. They were able to give their wives flowers, gifts, dinners out, weekend getaways, and vacations. For instance, my pastor vacationed with his family as often as twice a year, spent frequent getaway weekends with his wife, as well as provided her with gifts and fine clothes. Of course, for the average married man in our fellowship, the job description of a husband-and-father was spiritually, physically, and economically impossible. Since I could not afford those things, I had to imitate where I could.

One verse frequently quoted to reinforce the role of husband as provider of all the needs of his wife and family was 1 Timothy 5:8:

> If anyone does not provide for his relatives, and especially for his immediate family, he has denied the faith and is worse than an unbeliever.

Our interpretation was that if a husband could not provide a four-bedroom, two-and-a-half-bath home in a neighborhood with curbs, sidewalks, and underground utilities; two late-model cars; tuition for private school; and proper annual family vacations, without his wife being employed outside the home, he had denied the faith. No mention was ever made that this verse is completely surrounded by instruction to the church as to the care of widows. We had made another general principle out of a very specific statement—the result was disaster. Jehovah-jireh was removed as provider and replaced with Joe-husband. I was the provider of my family's needs, and in turn, I worshiped my work, which became my provider. I pretended to look to God, but trusted in my own strength, eventually travelling over 180 days some years. In doing so, I truly denied the faith.

In 1 Timothy 3:4 and 12, Paul required each overseer and deacon to "manage his own family well." Any husband who was unable to meet all his family's needs was presumed unfit for the ministry. A wife who wanted a good report for her husband was obliged to keep her problems to herself, or take them to her husband. To share a problem with a friend or to seek professional counseling would "uncover" her husband and would somehow be a reflection of his bad management. Husbands, also, had to be careful what family problems they shared with their personal pastors, since problems at home were thought to be instant disqualification for ministry.

Fatherpower   *Promise Keepers Views*

It was taught that the source of all physical and spiritual provision in the family was the father. Not only was the father "worshiped" in the family, he was considered the answer to the world's leadership problems, and was the exclusive means for the transmission of God's love. In his message "Fatherpower," Bob Mumford said:

> God's answer for the leadership crisis in our world today is the same as it was 3500 years ago—fathers! The only way God's love and fatherhood is going to come into this world is through men who know how to rule and father.[1]

In the shepherding movement, fathers were taught to be the exclusive source of "God's love and fatherhood" for the world. This overstatement was clearly a reaction to the anti-family direction of society, but combined with an authoritarian view of the church, this overemphasis on the father's role in the spiritual life of the family became serious error. In "Fatherpower" Mumford never mentions the work of the Son on the Cross in bringing the Father's love into the world two thousand years ago. This kind of emphasis (on the negative), and omission (of the positive) only served to distort the institution of the family and the role of the father.

The structural significance of the father's role was elevated to the exclusion of the Spirit's work. The father was to be the head of the home, not because he was qualified spiritually, but because he was the father. "Fatherpower" was taught without a hint of where the power to be an effective father comes from. The father's *position* was his qualification, and without an understanding of the dominion and work of the Holy Spirit in the home, families became the domain of the father.

Perhaps most damaging for the father was the notion that because he had the *position* of authority in the home, that automatically gave him the *ability* to "rule in God's name." The effect this misunderstanding had in me was spiritual laziness. I had been "anointed" in my role as a father—sufficient for all my family's needs because I had the position of father. The spiritual challenges of raising a family were easily deflected to structural concerns. What I said was law because I said it. My personal walk with God was not an issue. I learned to trust the structure of the family instead of trusting Christ. For me, this was idolatry. . .subtle, but idolatry just the same.

Because of my position (husbands were regarded as "popes," infallible because of their position), Vicki rarely challenged my decisions, even when she felt I was missing God's will. When we moved to Jacksonville, Vicki felt strongly that it was not the will of God. Given the structure of our marriage, I assumed I did not have to take her view as seriously as I took my own or my pastor's. This view was continuously reinforced. Men bragged that they had never washed dishes or changed a diaper. Wives testified to the "release" they felt when they turned over the spiritual needs of the home to their husbands though they were sometimes treated like children. Single women lived vicariously through their pastor and his family. Overt or subtle, abusive legalism resulted.

Wives, Submit Yourselves

Wives who tried to resist the frequent injustices of the system were subjected to intense peer pressure—most gave in. The few who did not were considered "unsubmissive" and dishonoring to their husbands.

Many couples either had to choose the lifeless structural standard or leave their relationship with God, since the structure was seen to be God's order for the home and was usually the choice.

One woman was counseled by the wife of a leader to submit to her husband in spite of his alcoholism and frequent adultery. Her submission enabled him to continue in his sin for several years without having to confront it.

As a church, we did not remain alone regarding our emphasis on submission of the wife to the husband. In recent years, Christian leaders, who twenty years ago were vehemently attacking our leaders for their stand, have found that it is popular to emphasize the submission issue. This change is doubtless in reaction to the anti-God, anti-male sentiment now prevalent in Western culture. One feminist writer defines marriage as "rape and lifelong slavery," while another accuses men of seizing power and control and forcing women into subservient roles by sentimentalizing her "role" as wife and mother.[2] But, reaction is not the same as redemption.

Emphasis on the submission of the wife was perceived as resistance to the aspects of our culture that would blur all distinctions between the sexes. We appeared to be raising a standard for Christ in the battle for the home.

The role of the godly mother in the spiritual life of the home was submerged in the leadership of the father. We were taught that in Christian society today women exercise control over the family and the local church by default because of the general spiritual apathy of men. Thus women were forced into positions of authority they were never created to fill. Men must therefore arise and take their rightful places of authority in the home and in the church if they were to be obedient to the Word of

God, and truly love their wives "as Christ loved the church."

Spiritual Institution

The shepherding movement, and much of the evangelical church today, made the family into an object of worship. A proper marriage relationship was considered the solution to or prevention of almost every problem of the individual Christian.

The relationship of a husband, wife, and children is not an ideal to be attained by faithfulness and right understanding. It is rather a divine reality, founded on fellowship with Jesus Christ. It is not therefore, a human institution. It cannot be expected to function properly without the personal presence of its founder. Any operational understanding of the home that begins with the role of the wife or husband is flawed.

The family exists through and in Jesus Christ. We imposed a human organizational model on what is essentially a spiritual institution. Human models require human effort, and yield fleshly results. Confusion, domination, and fear ruled where righteousness, peace, and joy in Christ's love should have reigned.

ACROSS THE GRAIN

A number of evangelicals have raised serious questions about the submission issue. A plain reading of Ephesians 5:22–33, Colossians 3:18, and 1 Peter 3:7 was enough for us. We always assumed that all real Christians would eventually see the great truths we had uncovered in the Scriptures for them. All that they really needed was the courage to obey the word of the Lord.

But the meanings of these passages are not nearly so obvious as we were taught. Problems with our view of the roles of each member of the home become clearer on close inspection. The main problem has to do with culture, since the culture we are in determines to a large extent how we understand what we read in the Scriptures.

For instance, some theologians are troubled that the New Testament does not specifically prohibit slavery. In fact, it seems to condone it. But the fact remains that over twenty centuries the gospel, everywhere it has gone, has had the effect of eventually eliminating slavery. Today, Christians in every culture repudiate it. Why? Because implicit in the gospel is the message of human liberty. The writers of the New Testament were addressing a fact of life in their culture, and their admonitions concerning the treatment of slaves were culture-bound. The gospel, however, is not bound by their culture.

Also implicit in the gospel is the sense of equality of all people before God. All have sinned, and all are equally in need of a Savior. All have been made righteous by the same blood. As is the accepted view of slavery being culturally based, could the New Testament instruction concerning women also have been tied to the culture?

Personally I have problems with interpretations that bind any part of Scripture exclusively to a time other than our own, thereby making it irrelevant for today. But that is not the case here. Understanding our culture and something of the culture being addressed reveals much about the meaning of Paul's words, which were radical for his times. We forget that our mind-set has been affected by democracy, abolition and labor reform, and women's suffrage.[3]

Ephesians 5 was directed primarily to husbands, not wives. While in verses 21, 24, and 33 wives are told to submit to their husbands in everything and to show respect to them, that was nothing new. Wives had heard that for generations! Radically new are Paul's words to husbands. In verse 21 he insists that husbands enter into a relationship of mutual submission with their wives. Twenty centuries later we can only imagine how revolutionary this new teaching was to the first hearers.[4]

We thought the idea of submission of wives to husbands was deeply spiritual because it cut across the grain of our culture. In fact, it is almost always the hallmark of pagan cultures! In a sense, we were guilty of imposing our modern, more egalitarian culture onto Paul's words. We interpreted the passage in a way that seemed counter to the secular direction of our culture. In reality, we arrived at a very different meaning from what Paul intended.

In Paul's culture, submission went only one way, from the wives to the husbands. But this was the old way. Christian marriage is to be characterized by the mutual submission of each partner to the other. The example has already been set by the head of the church, Christ (Eph. 5:25, 29). Out of reverence to him, we are to follow his example (v. 21).

Paul's teaching here actually lifted a wife in status to a position of equality with her husband. As in Titus 2:4–5 and Colossians 3:18, she could now love and subject herself to her husband as she always had—but now without fear of being used. In the context of the times, this new position for women was revolutionary.

The husband was no longer to be a tyrant, dominator, and controller. He was to have a relationship with his wife of love and self-giving after the pattern of Christ. The old authoritarian barriers had been removed. Looking at it this way, Ephesians 5:21–33 now fits with Galatians 3:28: "There is neither Jew nor Greek, slave nor free, male nor female, for you are all one in Christ Jesus."[5]

In Ephesians 5, Paul was undermining a hierarchical model of the home that was very similar to the one we created using his words! Paul calls all of us today, in our highly self-oriented society, to put the needs of others above our own. This has always gone against human understanding in every time and culture.

Headship

Another basis for our theology of the hierarchy of the home is the idea of the "headship" of the husband. However, headship as a hierarchical concept is not taught in the New Testament. From the example of the chairman of the board of General Motors being the "head" of the company and the "brains" of the outfit, we extrapolated that wives were the "bodies" and husbands were the "brains" of the home. We were guilty of applying twentieth-century understandings to Paul's language.

Paul's original readers did not have the slightest idea of the function of the brain and the nervous system. They attributed what we call mental functions to the soul, the spirit, or to other parts of the body like the heart, the bowels, the kidneys, and the bones. It was impossible for Paul to use the idea of head as being the center of control. Even if he had, his readers would never have understood.

Paul never used "head" in the same context as the idea of the church as the "body" of Christ (Rom. 12:4-8; 1 Cor. 12:12-31; Eph. 4:11-16; Col. 2:19). In 1 Corinthians 11:3, Ephesians 1:22, and Colossians 2:10 he speaks of a head without referring to a body, but he never once made the connection the way we did.

In fact, Paul used the two metaphors, head and body, to say two very different things. The idea of the body of Christ is used to explain the mutuality and interdependence of Christian relationships in the church. The head metaphor is used of Christ as the source and maintainer of the church. When our teachers brought the two metaphors together they changed the original meanings. They interpreted them in the light of modern science and read into them something that is not there![6]

What *does* Paul mean when he uses the term "head." We looked at headship as control, but Christ's headship was very different. His headship was expressed in the rest of the Ephesians 5 passage by his love, self-sacrifice, provision, nourishing, and cherishing of the church. For Christ, being head was not the same as being in charge. The self-emptying of Christ, described by Paul in Philippians 2:5, is all over this passage too. Paul is saying to husbands, "Your attitude should be the same as that of Christ Jesus." Just as Christ left his Father's house to give himself for the church, so the husband must leave the home of his parents and enter a relationship of commitment and mutual submission with his wife. This is how the relationship of husband and wife parallels the mystery of Christ and the church found in Ephesians 5:32. None of these actions or attitudes that Christ modeled involved the exercise of authority.[7]

Our modern understanding of anatomy has blinded us to the meaning of these passages. He isn't talking about management structure at all but about an entirely new way for two people to relate to one another.

The Order of Creation

Lip service was sometimes given to the idea of mutual submission, but only in the context of the home and as a chain of command. Genesis 2:18 and 20 is taught in the shepherding movement as describing "God's intended order of creation"—the hierarchial model of the husband-wife relationship: "The LORD God said, 'It is not good for the man to be alone. I will make a helper suitable for him.'" Man was created to rule over creation and woman was given as a "helper" who was "suitable," or "meet" for him. This creation order is supposedly being affirmed in Ephesians 5:22 with Paul allegedly commanding the Ephesians to return to the God-ordained model of wifely submission. Vicki and I felt that being my help-meet meant that her only purpose in life was to help me do what God had called me to do.

But there are problems with this understanding. The idea of subordination is not implied in the word used in Genesis. In Hebrew, an *ezer* is not an assistant in the sense of a subordinate whose role it is to carry out the wishes of a superior. Old Testament usage does not refer to the status of either the helper or the recipient. There is just the sense of one person coming to the aid of another. In fact, the term is frequently used of God, "We wait in hope for the Lord; he is our help (*ezer*) and our shield" (Ps. 33:20). The first indication that husbands will rule over their wives is in Genesis 3:16, and is one of the consequences of the Fall. Far from being the *created* order, the submission of wives to husbands is associated with the *fallen* order!

The Problem with Hierarchy

Eventually we all ask ourselves, "How did we get here? We started out as two people in love with the Lord and with each other. Now, we don't know about either one." Most of us face the loss of a sense of identity and a greatly weakened relationship with Jesus Christ. And it happened while we were emphasizing the importance of the family.

In our home, much of the mutual love and respect between husband and wife as persons was lost and replaced with an artificial relationship based on structural roles. It is much more difficult to manage a relationship of mutuality than one built on hierarchy. Real problems must be dealt with, real feelings expressed (in love of course), and each person's leadings from God must be taken into account.

Fulfilling roles has the effect of masking the personal

problems of the husband or wife. When families leave the church and allow for changes in structure unsolved personal problems surface, and, without outside understanding and help, pressures can be devastating. Blame is placed in all the wrong places. Those still committed to the structure blame the couple's withdrawal from fellowship. The couples who have left blame the church and the structure it represents.

Actually it was our unnatural, unscriptural way of relating together that hindered the Spirit's work of grace in our lives. The emotional healing, vitality, and spontaneity intended by God for the marriage relationship were all forced into the straitjacket of authority and submission.

The passage in Ephesians 5 relates the concepts of the home and the church. Our twisted understanding of marriage and the home not only distorted how we related to one another at home, but also how we related to each other and to God. We sowed the bad seed of bad ideas, and reaped bitter fruit.

9

THE ROOT OF THE PROBLEM

One consequence of dysfunctional families is that they produce children who are unable to trust God, or anyone else. The same is true of dysfunctional "spiritual families."

LORDSHIP

Lordship of Jesus Christ in the life of the believer was the espoused aim of the teachings and practices of the shepherding movement. The believer, after implementing both the doctrine of authority in the church and the teaching on complete submission and total commitment to a personal pastor into everyday life, was supposed to be enabled to submit to and live daily under Christ's rule in every area of life. This is a noble-sounding goal in these times of easy believism and cheap grace. The church can always benefit from a deeper understanding of Christ's Lordship—unless that understanding obscures all other knowledge of our relationship to him.

There are many titles given to Jesus in the Bible. Each one of them is packed with implications that affect our conduct and character. We knew him only as Lord, Master, King, and Shepherd. But he is also Self-Giving

Savior, Wisdom, Sustainer of Life, Heart's Delight, Binder of Wounds, Dresser of Nature, Searcher for a Lost Coin, Tender Forgiver, Compassionate Giver, Companion in Sorrow, Teacher of Peace, Son, Firstborn Among Many Brethren, Friend. Any of these titles taken without the others, as the whole picture of who Jesus is, distorts our vision of him and ourselves. If we are to understand what it means to say "Jesus is Lord," we must take his other titles into account.

I have recently realized that my devotional life was limited solely to worship. Christ's authority, majesty, wonder, might, power, and wisdom were the only attributes that I considered. His goodness, patience, grace, mercy, and love were not so evident to me as I worshiped in church. The worship was wonderful—so wonderful that I rarely felt the need to seek him devotionally. Praise, thanksgiving, petitions, and intercession were the extent of my prayer life. I am learning that there are times when I pray that he just wants to hold me and love me. He is always worthy of praise but he is becoming much more to me than simply "Lord."

What kind of lordship does Jesus have? It may help to see the kind of lordship he forbids.

The word translated "to lord it over" appears in Matthew 20:25–26, Mark 10:42–43, Luke 22:25–26, and in 1 Peter 5:2–3. Actually the word does not suggest oppression or abuse of power. It simply means "to rule over" or "to be lord over." Coercion or the abuse of authority is not the issue here. What is being said is that there is among the Gentiles a hierarchical system of authority that is not to be imitated in the Christian community.[1]

The passage in Luke 22:25, makes the issue even clearer. Jesus says, ". . .and those who exercise authority over them call themselves Benefactors." The term was an honorary title given in gratitude by the one who had received favor, acknowledging himself as inferior in status to the benefactor. Among the Gentiles, rule was connected with status. What was expressly forbidden was the Gentile practice of ruling from a position of elevated status or bestowed honor.[2]

Husbands, pastors, and church leaders in the shepherding movement came into their positions by marriage, appointment, or gifting. Once in their "place" of authority, others were to submit to them out of respect for their position—regardless of their fitness—in the fear that resisting them was resisting God. This is the same pagan concept of rule by status prohibited by Jesus himself.

Our leaders supported the idea of status rule by using the example of Paul's appeal to Philemon. Paul could, as an apostle, have ordered Philemon to accept and forgive Onesimus. Instead, Paul graciously laid aside his authority as an apostle in order to appeal to Philemon to willingly obey out of love. But, if the notion of Paul's exalted status is not brought to the text, a different picture emerges. "Therefore, although in Christ I could be bold and order you to do what you ought to do, yet I appeal to you on the basis of love" (Philem. 8–9). Paul was able to give an order to Philemon "in Christ" because they are both Christians. There is no appeal to his apostolic authority in this text. Further, in Christ, he could order Philemon only to do what he "ought to do" as a Christian. Paul is not saying he could order Philemon to obey his wishes if he wanted to because he is an apostle. As a Christian and an apostle, the only thing Paul could require was that another Christian do his Christian duty.

Paul continues to erode the idea of rule by status in verse 17: "So if you consider me a partner, welcome him as you would welcome me." Paul places himself in a relationship of mutuality not only with Philemon but also with Onesimus his slave!

DISCIPLESHIP AND CHURCH GOVERNMENT

No form of church government is convincingly presented in the New Testament. That is why people impose their own customs on the church and why there are hundreds of forms of church polity. That is exactly what those of us in the shepherding movement did. Our church was organized in pyramid fashion in direct contradiction to the principle that Paul encouraged. The pastor-disciple relationship was the mortar that held our church structure together. The follower was discipled by his pastor who was discipled by his pastor—all the way to Charles Simpson or one of the other teachers at the top. The problem is that all earthly models of organization reveal their fallenness when superimposed on the church.

The Military Model

Military models of organization and obedience are often used to teach this personal form of discipleship. One of the most carefully organized armies in history, the Roman army, was present everywhere the Gospels and Paul's letters were circulated. If military organization and obedience were the basis for understanding discipleship and church government, there would have been numerous examples in everyday life for the writers of the New Testament to have drawn upon. This was not the case though, in his letter to the Christians at the Roman military colony of Philippi, Paul uses several military expressions—not one of which refers to the Roman army's chain of command.

Instead, the New Testament gives only one example, that of Jesus' appreciation of the centurion's understanding of the nature of his authority. The central theme of this encounter is Jesus' recognition, in front of unbelieving Jews, of a Gentile's faith in God. A Gentile, worse yet a Roman official, recognized and trusted Jesus' authority when the Jews, who were supposed to be spiritual, refused. This example is not support for a system of church authority, but is rather an encouragement for us to believe Jesus when he gives us his word. No military model of church government is supported by the New Testament.

Delegated Authority

What about the shepherding movement's now infamous doctrine of "delegated authority"? When the military model of authority is removed from our understanding of Jesus and his ministry, we get a very different picture of Jesus' authority and lordship, and it is vastly different from what we see in twentieth-century western culture. Earthly "lords" and leaders extend their rule by delegating their authority to subordinates.

Jesus' authority was never delegated in the sense that it became another's authority. Matthew 28:18 says: "All authority in heaven and on earth has been given to me. Therefore go. . . ." We are commanded to go and make disciples because he has all authority. He did not say, "All authority has been given to me and now I'm going to give you some." We are commanded to "disciple all nations," specifically by going, baptizing, and teaching them to observe all that Jesus commands us to do. No authorization whatever is given to make them observe our commands. "All authority in heaven and earth" remains his and his alone.

In Matthew 10:1, Jesus gave his disciples authority "to drive out evil spirits and to cure every kind of disease and sickness." This delegation of authority was clearly intended to continue after Jesus' ascension and is extended in the book of Acts to those other than "the twelve." But this authority is to be over sickness and evil spirits—not over people, as those in the shepherding movement leadership taught. Jesus never delegated his authority over his disciples to anyone. Paul subjected himself to this limitation by never once insisting that individual believers obey his words in personal matters not related to the gospel or sin.

The Joint That Supplies

Charles Simpson and the other teachers applied the biblical references of hierarchical authority to the metaphor of the church as Christ's body:

> When the Bible describes the church as his Body, it is using an analogy to teach us about the nature of the church. While any analogy or parable has limitations, we can see some valid comparisons. First, God's people are to be related by joints. Just as the members of a physical body are related by joints, so the church, a many-membered body, is related by joints. This conclusion is not only implied in the Body analogy, but specifically stated in Scripture: "From whom the whole body, being fitted and held together by that which every joint supplies, according to the proper working of each individual part, causes the growth of the body for the building up of itself in love" (Eph. 4:16 NASB).
>
> The Spirit, the life of the body, is invisible. But the Body itself is the visible manifestation of the Spirit of God. The Body is not only visible to God, but to the world as well. The world is to behold its behavior and glorify God (1 Pet. 2:12). . . .
>
> Such a visible, literal Body requires literal and visible joints. But these joints must be functional, not merely theoretical or mystical. A mystical Body with mystical joints will never make a spiritually blind world say, "Glory to God."[3]

The combination of the other things we had been taught along with this analogy meant, to us, that our network of committed relationships became the "visible manifestation of the Spirit of God." With the body analogy as the basis of our movement, we concluded that ours was obviously the only form of church government specifically authorized by Scripture.

> Without joints, the body would become as Ezekiel's vision of dry bones, the scattered memory of a once-great army. The first step in restoration is "bone must come to his bone" (Ezek. 37:7). To put it another way, the right people must get together in the right way to function in God's purpose under Jesus' headship. The enemy of the church is not the diversity that is within it, but rather the lack of sufficiently strong joints to hold the members in place together as they supply out of their God-given uniqueness. Strong commitment, member to member, is required before there is the freedom to function in a free-flowing life of truth and love. Strong edification and correction can only come in a atmosphere preconditioned by covenant commitment.[4]

The fallacy here is the exclusive focus on the structural nature of joints. The problem with the bones in Ezekiel's vision was not their lack of correct structural relationships. The problem was they were dead. And they were dead because they were without God's Spirit.

As admitted by Simpson in the article cited above, there are problems with any analogy that is taken too far. Examples given in the article imply that there is a hierarchical arrangement in the church that begins at the head and proceeds from one joint to another to the extremities. This was how I understood the arrangement and this was how our church was organized.

But, as we saw in the last chapter, twentieth-century interpretations of Paul's body metaphors are fraught with problems. Neither he nor his original readers understood "head" as being "control center." The image of the head meant something more like "source" or "headwaters," and spoke of Christ's beginning, saving, and sustaining the church. In the same way, "body" spoke of the mutual interdependence of all Christians.

Paul's use of the body metaphor described a mutually

related community with Christ as its creator and sustainer. The idea of the body of Christ as being a hierarchically
developed organism is not taught in the New Testament.
Further, Jesus used the analogy of the vine and the
branches to illustrate the relationship between himself
and his church. "I am the vine; you are the branches. If a
man remains in me and I in him, he will bear much fruit;
apart from me you can do nothing" (John 15:5). This
analogy erodes the shepherding movement's notion that
their hierarchial structure was biblical. The only joint that
supplies is Jesus Christ.

The Linchpin

The linchpin of the shepherding movement and other
similar groups and organizations is the concept of a
"committed relationship" to a "personal pastor" or "disci-
pler." The orthodoxy, or that which was taught on this
issue, was not orthodox at all. This doctrine has caused
great pain and confusion for many followers and also for
many of its proponents. The reason for the pain is
simple—the doctrine is false! It is another gospel, usurping the rightful place of Jesus Christ in the life of the
follower and obscuring the regenerating, sanctifying work
of the Cross in his or her life.

The "personal pastor doctrine," like so many of the
other distinctive teachings of the shepherding movement,
is not supported by Scripture. We practiced a form of
Christianity not found in the Bible. We will examine the
Scriptures we used to see if they actually teach what we
practiced.

Commitment

The extent of the pastor's authority in the life of the
follower was total. Commitment to total obedience to the

pastor's word on the part of the follower was the means by which this authority was exercised. It was seen as the means to the end regarding the total lordship of Jesus Christ in the life of the believer. In the March, 1974 issue of *New Wine Magazine*, in answer to the question, "What should be the degree of a commitment to someone who is 'discipling' you?" Charles Simpson says:

> If the disciple is ready to give his life to the Lord, he will "lay it at the apostles feet"—completely. One cannot lay his life and possessions down for God, unless he does it unto God's government to which he is related. Every commitment should be considered permanent. Any commitment made with reservations or stipulation is not total.[5]

If a disciple had really given his life to the Lord, he would lay his life and possessions at the feet of those in church government for them to use and direct as they saw fit. That was what it meant to me; it was what was expected of me, and that was exactly what I did—to the best of my ability.

But this was not what actually happened in Acts 4:35, the verse apparently alluded to in the statement quoted above. Beginning in verse 34b we find:

> For from time to time those who owned lands or houses sold them, brought the money from the sales and put it at the apostles' feet, and it was distributed to anyone as he had need.

In Acts 5:4 we find that this was clearly not the expected conduct for believers. It was not even an all-inclusive practice, only as many as had houses and lands. The revenue was not completely at the apostles' disposal, it was to be distributed as anyone had need. Not all possessions were included in these sales, only houses and lands, the rest were regarded as common property with all other believers, not just the apostles (4:32).

The picture here clearly is not one of believers totally

committing their lives to the apostles, but rather of believers wonderfully committing what they could to each other because of their total commitment to Jesus. Our leaders alluded to a verse of Scripture to support a practice that was not intended by the context.

Church Leaders

Leaders of the New Testament church never gave personal advice and direction to individual followers. Not once in Scripture is a follower exhorted to obey the personal advice or direction of a church leader, except where sin or a question regarding the gospel is at issue. Paul's concern and advice for Timothy's stomach in 1 Timothy 5:23 is hardly a foundation upon which to build a system of life and conduct. While Paul seems to give advice in 1 Timothy 2:9 and Peter in 1 Peter 3:3 concerning the braiding of the hair, it is a general command and is not directed toward a specific individual. In Peter's case, the theological foundation for his command is the issue, not Peter's authority. Other commands in the New Testament that appear to be directed toward individuals always have to do with sin.

Probably the most revealing example of a person who did not give personal advice is that of Jesus himself. He is not seen giving personal advice, direction, or requiring unquestioning obedience from anyone as a prerequisite for acceptance as a disciple—unless sin or following him was involved. Jesus' conduct was, and now the Holy Spirit's is, never to exercise control over believers on the basis of their commitments.

Jesus reveals his low regard for commitments in Matthew 26:33–35. Peter and the disciples had committed themselves to die with Jesus before they would disown him. But Jesus told them the truth because he knew their limitations. Jesus' ability to disciple Peter and the rest and later make them witnesses, did not rest on their ability to keep a commitment, but upon God's grace about to be won for them on Calvary.

Great Commission

In what we know as the "Great Commission passage" found in Matthew 28:19–20, Jesus commands his disciples to make disciples of all nations. Yet not once does a disciple of Jesus speak of another believer as being "my disciple." Paul and Timothy's relationship was also often used in the shepherding movement to illustrate personal discipling relationships, but Paul never refers to Timothy as "my disciple." In fact, in Acts 16:1 before Timothy ever meets Paul, Timothy is already described as being "a disciple."

The book of Acts only once uses the posessive with regard to disciples. Shortly after his conversion, Paul was helped to escape from Damascus by his disciples (Acts 9:25 NASB). Evidently as a former student of Gamaliel, Paul gathered followers around himself as Gamaliel did. He later repudiated the practice in Acts 20:30. At no other time are disciples referred to as Paul's disciples or Barnabas' disciples, or anybody's disciples. I am not raising an issue of semantics. Jesus' relationship to his disciples was unique, and was never duplicated by the first recipients of the Great Commission or the eyewitnesses of the ascension. The first generation of disciple-makers did not take disciples after themselves, even though it was the standard practice of the day. Yet, throughout the book of Acts, believers are referred to as "disciples." Jesus' relationship with his disciples was apparently not the model for making disciples in the New Testament. This understanding is crucial if we are ever to know the meaning of the Great Commission.

Submission

Complete submission to the will of man was considered a necessary prerequisite to being discipled.

> Others will draw back because they are willing to "submit to God," but they were not willing to "submit to man." The Scripture teaches us that man is a rebel. When the Lordship of Jesus truly conquers a man's self-management, the Lordship of Jesus is manifest by his now submissive and meek spirit (1 Cor. 11:1–3; Eph. 5:22–32; 6:1–3; Phil. 2:5–15; Col. 3:18–25; 1 Thess. 5:12–14; 1 Tim. 3:4–5, 12; Heb. 13:7, 17). *[References to wives submitting to husbands, slaves to masters, and members to leaders, plural.]* A submissive or meek person is not weak, but bridled. It is interesting that in 1 Peter 5:5–6 humbling oneself under elders is equated with humbling oneself under the mighty hand of God.[6]

First Peter 5:5–6 is said to teach that submission to elders is the same as submission to God.

> The question is not whether to submit, it is where to submit. . . . Wherever and whenever, submission must be done with the conviction that God has led you into it, and therefore you are relating to your leader as unto the Lord. The decision should bring peace and joy. The relationship as a disciple is not contrived or strained. His yoke is easy and his burden is light—but his yoke is a yoke.[7]

The conclusion is that if a believer is under the lordship of Jesus, he will seek a leader, singular, and submit to him as unto the Lord. First Peter 5:5–6 is the only Scripture that was given as making this connection in this leader-follower context. But the context, beginning in verse one, appears to make a different point:

> [1] To the elders among you, I appeal as a fellow elder, a witness of Christ's sufferings and one who also will share in the glory to be revealed: [2] Be shepherds of God's flock that is under your care, serving as overseers—not because you must, but because you are willing. . .[3] not lording it over those entrusted to you, but being examples to the flock.

> [4] And when the Chief Shepherd appears, you will receive the crown of glory that will never fade away.
>
> [5] Young men, in the same way be submissive to those who are older. All of you, clothe yourselves with humility toward one another, because,
>
> > "God opposes the proud
> > but gives grace to the humble."
>
> [6] Humble yourselves, therefore under God's mighty hand, that he may lift you up in due time. [7] Cast all your anxiety on him because he cares for you.

The equating of young men's submission to elders with humbling themselves under God's mighty hand, "as unto the Lord," is not clear at all. The limiting factor for young men being submissive to those who are older is Peter's command in verse 5b, "with humility toward one another." This is a prohibition of strict one-way submission and appears to reemphasize Peter's instruction to elders not to rule over those entrusted to them from a position of higher status (v. 3).

The phrase, "Humble yourselves, therefore," (v. 6) clearly refers the reader back to "because God is opposed to the proud. . . ." Peter is using Proverbs 3:34 to support his command for all to humble themselves under the mighty hand of God because God is opposed to the proud. This command is not directed to the relationship between young men and elders, but to the whole church.

This passage does not make "humbling oneself under the elders" and "humbling oneself under the mighty hand of God" equal. The statement "you are relating to your leader as unto the Lord," which was made by Charles Simpson, is not supported by this passage. In fact, the passage as a whole prohibits the kind of total submission Simpson called for and we practiced. Our doctrine of "submitting to elders as unto the Lord" was forced onto a scripture that does not teach it.

In the New Testament, believers in Jesus are asked,

as a general principle, to submit to church leadership—leadership that is always made up of more than one person. No individual New Testament believer is ever required to make a total commitment, without stipulation or condition, to another believer as Simpson required (see note 6). Honor and obedience without stipulation or condition can only rightfully be given to Jesus himself. "If anyone comes to me, and does not hate his father and mother, his wife and children, his brothers and sisters—yes, even his own life—he cannot be my disciple" (Luke 14:26). Attempting total commitment to Jesus and total commitment to anyone or anything else only confirms Jesus' observation in Matthew 6:24, "No one can serve two masters. Either he will hate the one and love the other, or he will be devoted to the one and despise the other. . . ."

There are two real dangers in giving or receiving a commitment such as we did. First, like it or not, love for and commitment to Jesus will almost always be the loser. It is just easier to love and submit to someone you can see. Second, by making a commitment, without stipulation or condition, we gave over what amounts to total control of our lives to a human leader. By giving advice or direction, the leader *exercised* control over our lives. When this advice or direction went against our conscience, and we obeyed anyway, our behavior was manipulated. Regardless of the intentions of either the followers or disciplers, this unholy connection of control between human beings is the moral, ethical, and biblical equivalent of witchcraft.

ALL THE WAY TO THE TOP

The doctrines of "complete submission," and "total commitment" to another human being caused untold misery and lasting damage to the spiritual lives of thousands. It may help you to know that the problems were not isolated to your own group; they went all the way to the top.

To many of us, the concepts of "pastor," "discipleship," and "covenant" have lost the lofty meanings ascribed to them in Scripture. They have become ugly reminders of the past and are laden with painful associations. It has become clear to us that, if we who have been damaged by this or any similar practice of discipleship are to move on and return to a life characterized by the fruit of the Spirit, then telling our stories and identifying the problems of distorted or misapplied truth is not enough. We must identify the root of the problem.

The following is not an attempt to impugn the character of any person or group of persons. Conduct not in keeping with one's character or profession is not criminal, but simply a reminder of our fallen humanity. What we are about to say is not to accuse or even to correct those who were in leadership, but hopefully to bring light to those in darkness. Please do not confuse our bluntness with a lack of Christian charity.

I am aware that there are many who opposed our teachers (whose commitment to each other brought about a movement based on personal disciple-making). There is no room for you to read this and say, "I told you so." The truth being told here does not vindicate you—it is for those who suffer today in their walk with God because of chronic emotional and psychological abuse perpetrated on them in the name of discipleship. Only the truth can make them free.

DO AS WE SAY

In his 1986 book *Challenge to Care*, Charles Simpson states: "The biblical pattern is that pastors, elders, bishops, whatever their description, function together. In so doing not only are they protected but so are their constituents.'[8] The teachers listed in chapter 1 certainly fit this description. Clearly they had no other relationships that could offer this kind of protection. A board made up of those they were discipling, or shepherding could hardly suffice. Yet in the August 1987, issue of *Charisma*, Ben Gehezzi reports:

> Their long-standing covenant brotherhood had been largely positive, supportive and mutually beneficial. But building covenant relationships is always fraught with complexities and problems, and the five teachers and their families were no exception.
>
> Submitting to any community relationship naturally involves accepting limits that may be personally quite costly to the individual. This was a painful reality for the five men, whose gifts had made each a spiritual powerhouse. For example, the men had agreed to submit their speaking and travel plans for mutual discernment, a decision that came to be a nagging source of frustration.[9]

Clearly, the scheduling requirements of their personal careers began to take precedence over consistent submitted fellowship with the only ones to whom they could really be accountable. Bob Mumford is quoted in the same Charisma article as saying:

> The fruit of those fifteen years has been a very great blessing mixed with some very real pain. At the end of that time, I recognized more clearly that something was not right. As we discussed our relationship, the four of us decided that if we were to take our places of ministry in the wider body of Christ, we had to dissolve our tight personal commitments.[10]

Charles Simpson stated in the October 1986 issue of *New Wine Magazine*:

> Just as *New Wine Magazine* was a significant factor in our original joining together, it has also been a significant symbol of our joint ministries and our corporate struc-

ture. . . . The truth is we believe that *New Wine Magazine* is a symbol of something God is instructing us to lay down. We believe He is calling us to a new season of His work in the church and the world.[11]

This was not obedience to God as it related to a deeper level of service to the body of Christ nor a problem with matching calenders. They were choosing not to follow their own teaching. They demonstrated to the world that they were unwilling to require of themselves the same level of commitment expected of their followers. The fact that they were "spiritual powerhouses" does not excuse their conduct—it makes it all the more deplorable. As Charles Simpson related in a *New Wine Magazine* article in September, 1985:

When I was a boy, I worked for a man who had me digging a sewer. He was not a churchgoer, but nevertheless, he was a hard worker. My father, a minister, wanted me to work for him so that I would learn to be diligent. One of our church members saw me digging the sewer line and complained to my boss that such work was beneath the dignity of a minister's son. He replied, "I don't ask that boy to do anything I don't do myself."[12]

Unfortunately, our leaders were not like the boss in the above example. Unwilling to remain in submitted relationships to each other, they continued to require the practice from us, their followers. Thousands of men and women gave up, and continue to give up, family relationships, promising careers, businesses, farms, and fruitful ministries in order to be in committed relationships primarily because of the teaching and supposed example of these men.

The leaders ended their "committed" relationships because, as Bob Mumford admitted above, "something was not right." That "something" was that submitting to each other went against everything else they believed about the Scriptures and their walk with God. They ended their relationship of submission because it hindered the rest of their God-given ministry. However, what they taught about their relationship continues to hinder other God-given ministries, all over the world.

REALITY

The bluntness of the above is not intended to be hurtful, but we feel it is necessary to expose the root of the problem. Many of us who left the movement, left disappointed with ourselves, with the leadership, and with God. We are hurt and angry now, and we don't know why. We no longer want to go to church—any church.

If all these doctrines were false, what are we left with? Only Jesus Christ, his Cross, and an empty tomb. Our resurrection can come only after we have been to the foot of his Cross.

10

THE FIRST LOVE

HELP

Our experience in the discipleship movement has left us with a vague inner feeling of discontent and an indefinite desire for spiritual things. Our lives have tended to stagnate into what can be called "a generalized melancholy." We often hear ourselves say:

- "I am not very happy."
- "I am not content with the way my life is going."
- "I am not really joyful or peaceful, but I just don't know how things can be different."
- "I guess I have to be realistic and accept my life as it is."

This mood of resignation prevents us from actively searching for the life of the Spirit.[1]

Maybe that's just as well. After all it was a desire for deeper things of the Spirit that got us into this mess in the first place. It probably seems easier just to be numb and go on with the rest of our lives as if nothing had ever happened. We thought that maybe we would be able to put it behind us and go on. But, anyone still reading this book, especially this close to the end, has, like the rest of us, just not been able to do it.

Vicki and I were used to quick fixes. We were told, "You just need to do. . ." "Just listen to this. . ." "You need to read this. . ." or the really big one, "You really shouldn't feel that way about it." All we had to do was learn something new and we would get better, feel better, do better, and look better. So, if your experience has been anything like ours, you have a huge reservoir of information without any way to tie it to real life.

We learned to do what we were told, and we learned well. However, in the process, the chance to feel our own feelings and take our own actions was denied us. So we stopped taking any action. We waited to be told what to do. Now a great gulf separates what we know from what we do. We do not have another quick fix. We were in the movement for over fifteen years and it has taken time and trouble to get out of it and begin to get it out of us.

The last three chapters exposed some of the mistaken ideas we believed. These ideas distorted how you and we view ourselves. But there were basics, almost never taught about, that we share with all other Christians through the ages. These are the things we are going to have to cling to if we are ever going to be able to live with ourselves, enjoy being with other Christians, and, ultimately, enjoy being with God.

Much of what is said below was seldom, if ever, mentioned in the preaching, teaching, or publications of the shepherding movement. In our zeal to get at "what God is saying to the church today," we missed the main thrust of what he has been saying for two thousand years. The "gospel of the government of God" got us into this mess, but the Gospel of Jesus Christ is able to get us out.

THE CROSS

The Cross is the centerpiece of Christianity—not relationships, not even the church. In the shepherding movement, the Cross was viewed as the place to go to for new birth, and the community was the place to go to for new life. The Cross was where we found faith to obey God. The community was where that faith was worked out in obedience to men. Our provision in Christ in the shepherding movement was viewed as a mixture of Cross and community.

That mixture—more community than Cross—diluted the message of the Cross. The Cross of Jesus is our complete provision. The Cross is totally sufficient. The Cross is our only basis for receiving anything from God. Community should only be a part of the provision of the Cross that helps us maintain our new life before the world. In our case, we obeyed all we were told, did all we knew to do, and we were disappointed. We looked to the community for what the Cross alone can supply. Later we rejected a dysfunctional community and depended on our personal relationship with Jesus to qualify us for God's help—and were disappointed. We have suffered so much that we feel God really should help us and yet it seems he does not. What made the difference for us was a renewal of our understanding of what happened on the Cross.

THE EXCHANGE OF CALVARY

The Cross of Christ is the inexhaustible exchange of Calvary.[2]

All the evil that was due us was put on Jesus	So that all the good due Jesus could be given to us
He was punished for our sins	So that we could be forgiven

He was wounded	So that we could be healed
He was made sin with our sinfulness	So that we could be made righteous by his righteousness
He died our death	So that we could have eternal life
He became a curse for us	So that we could have the blessing that was due Him
He became poor with our poverty	So that we could be made rich with His riches

His poverty was total. In the same way, all his other suffering is also total. Total poverty can be defined as hunger, thirst, and need for all things.

- *He was hungry.* The Gospels indicate that, by the time Jesus was on the Cross, he had not eaten for about thirty-six hours.
- *He was thirsty.* His last words were "I thirst."
- *He was naked.* His garment had been taken from him and had been divided among the soldiers.
- *He was in need of all things.* He was buried in a borrowed grave, wrapped in a borrowed gown. On the Cross Jesus possessed nothing.

Just as literally as he endured our poverty:

He endured our shame	So that we could receive His Glory
He endured our rejection	So that we don't have to be rejected anymore. We are accepted the way Jesus was accepted, as God's children

We must decide if our lives will continue to be shaped by what was done to us in the church or by what Jesus did for us on the cross. There is no easy solution. By now you know only too well that nothing is easy. There are many barriers in our lives that keep us from the Cross. But God has removed every barrier on his side through Jesus' death and resurrection. The barriers that are in place are the ones we erected and we can, with God's grace, pull them down.

Can you identify with any of the experiences we shared in this book? Do you remember the sting of that first callous comment? The one that made you feel like you were a child. I remember thinking, "He must think I am a complete idiot to feel he has to say that to me." There were plenty of times like that and I got used to it. We have to face our feelings about what has been said and done to us by people we loved. Vertical pastoral relationships resulted in very twisted ways of relating to one another. We pursued close relationships, but found ourselves in loose associations with people who should have been our friends, but who could not be "friendly" because they were "in authority."

One of the hardest things I have ever had to do is admit that I was abused. The pastors I had through the years were not mean or evil men. I have heard stories and have seen other pastors abuse their followers, but none of that ever happened to me. I found, though, that I was walking through life almost numb—so numb, in fact, that a bottle of sparkling grape juice stayed in our refrigerator for two years awaiting a special occasion that never came. I was unable to feel strongly about anything. Some people get angry, some cry, but I felt numb.

FORGIVENESS

Forgiving Others

Forgiveness is for the benefit of those giving it, not for the benefit of those receiving it. It unhooks us from those who have hurt us and to some extent still control parts of our lives. It may seem that the Christian thing to do would be to take the blame ourselves, thinking, "No one forced us into this—we were grown-ups. We allowed this to happen. We are not victims." But it is really not that simple. If what we were taught had been true, every follower of Jesus Christ who wanted to follow him more nearly and love him more dearly would have joined. Our way of living the Christian life really seemed to be closest to the way it was in Acts 2:42, "They devoted themselves to the apostles' teaching and to the fellowship, to the breaking of bread and to prayer. Everyone was filled with awe, and many wonders and miraculous signs were done by the apostles." The leaders taught so convincingly that five councils of Christian leaders never recognized that it was the doctrines and not just their application that was causing the abuse.

The teaching of the movement sets us up to accept the most ridiculous treatment in the name of discipleship and Christian nurture. Because of our pastors and the teachers, years of our lives have been ruined and wasted. Whether they knew what they were doing to us spiritually or not will never change what we have been through.

After the initial numbness wears off, anger is the first appropriate response to the spiritual abyss and distorted fellowship we experienced. Discovery of the hypocrisy of our idea of fellowship has led to a sense of profound disappointment. The life we had surrounded ourselves with has now been exposed as an illusion. Those who claimed to have loved us were, in actuality, only doing their duty as good shepherds. We were their disciples— not real people.

Discovery of the hypocrisy or our idea of fellowship leads to profound disappointment. Where are all our "close" relationships now? Why didn't they last through the hard times? Does our partner love us for our own sake or just because that is his or her role in the marriage relationship? So much of what we had was empty and cheap. Rage is what happens in our soul when it awakens from living a lie. It doesn't help to deny how we feel. There are very valid reasons for how we feel.

After the anger, comes grief. Years of wholeness, joy of life, and usefulness to God are gone forever, and we grieve for them. In the middle of the sorrow and grief, in God's time and with his grace, we are able to forgive.[3]

We forgive because, through Jesus' work on the Cross, we have been forgiven. This forgiveness was won for us before we were even born, and is available even if we never accept it. Jesus taught his disciples to pray, "Forgive us our sins, for we also forgive everyone who sins against us" (Luke 11:4). Literally, "everyone who sins against us" means "the ones owing us." It is as if we hold IOUs upon which is stated what they have done to us. Forgiveness means we are to tear up the IOUs. Our forgiveness must follow the example God has given us—it must be unconditional.

God's forgiveness is different from that which is found in polite Western society. For example, if I do something that hurts you I am supposed to say, "I'm sorry, please forgive me." If you have good manners, you are supposed to say, "Apology accepted, I forgive you." This little exchange is supposed to keep the wheels of human relationships greased and running smoothly. But this kind of apology does not impress God. We really have no right to even ask for the kind of forgiveness we need. God has given forgiveness to us as a free gift.

There are several words that could have been used in the original language of the New Testament to describe what we are being asked to do. One means "to let pass" and is never used in this context. All of the other words used mean "to let go," "release," "pardon," or "cancel." These are all action words that have nothing to do with our polite forgive-and-forget, live-and-let-live mentality, but rather require us to *do* something—actively forgive—not just shrug it off. When we forgive we are not saying that what happened to us and others was all right. It was not all right. It was sin, against us and against God.

God's forgiveness of us was not primarily emotional. It was a decision of his will that apparently did not affect his emotions about our sin. He still hates it. But, his decision put us in a place of acceptance before him. Forgiveness is not an emotion, it is a decision, based on facts, not feelings. Forgiving is a decision only we can make. Changing our feelings is something only God can do. Forgiveness is a process that begins with our decision in response to God's forgiveness of us and continues as God heals the damage. It is not a quick fix. We decide in a moment, but the healing process may last for years.

The only sure basis for our being able to forgive those who have hurt us is the fact that we, ourselves, are forgiven. Any excuse we try make for those who have wronged us is inadequate—there is no excuse for what they did. If we say to ourselves, "They were deceived," or "They didn't know what they were doing," unforgiveness will creep back in.

We don't give excuses when we confess our sin to God, we just confess. Therefore, we don't give explanations why we are forgiving, we just forgive. It is a decision based on the fact of our forgiveness in Christ. Our decision to forgive is not based on their qualifications. We forgive even if we know they're not sorry. (What has been done to us is beyond "I'm sorry.") We forgive even if they did not ask for it. We forgive not so they will change; we forgive even when we know they won't change. We forgive even knowing they are still hurting others. We forgive even if they are going on with God without us. This is most difficult, especially when it seems God does not care what they did to us.

Forgiving God

We have been talking about forgiving others, but there are two other aspects to forgiveness—forgiving God and forgiving ourselves. God was there; he knew what was going on. Why didn't he do something? Why does he just let them go on like that? Why does it still hurt after all these years? If you were like us, you were only trying to do what you thought was his will when you got into all this. Why didn't he just lead in another direction? I would have been open, wouldn't you? In the preparation of this book, we have heard some very good reasons why people are not willing to trust God. Most of us feel we followed him into places where we were hurt and used. We all have good reasons to be angry at God and we need to realize he already knows how we really feel.

We do not have to understand everything. As with others, we decide to forgive God because we have been forgiven. Forgiving God increases our ability to trust him. I have found I can pray and trust God for miracles for everyone else, but when it comes to me, I just cannot believe him. I cannot believe he is going to provide for me. Sound familiar?

We have all heard all we want to hear about living by faith, but the kind of unbelief we have had to deal with is a fundamental lack of trust that God is good and that he will be good to us. This belief has been the hardest barrier for us to overcome. We are not the first people to feel this way. In Deuteronomy 1:27, the Israelites said, "The LORD hates us; so he brought us out of Egypt to deliver us into the hands of the Amorites to destroy us." It was not true, but that is what it looked like to them and that is how they felt. We do not have to make the same mistake. The Bible calls unbelief sin. When we decide to forgive God, we can then confess our unbelief and receive his cleansing from it. In the previous three chapters we have tried to show the corruption that was in so much of the teaching we received. This was man's teaching, not God's. God was not the author of your pain. He can be trusted.

Ourselves

Finally, we need to forgive ourselves. We have let ourselves down. Why were we so stupid? Why did we believe the teachers? Why didn't we leave at the first sign of error and abuse? Why did we let it happen? Why did we let it go on so long? Why didn't I stand up and say something? I knew exactly what I was doing, but I did it anyway. We direct our anger toward ourselves. Anger, while being an essential part of the process, will not ultimately bring healing. Remaining in anger and self-hatred only leads to more emptiness, depression, and a fatalistic attitude: "Nobody cares so why should I?"

We must forgive ourselves—not because we deserve it, not because we will never make another mistake—but because God has forgiven us. In the shepherding movement we were accepted based on our ability to perform, our external appearance. But God accepts us just like we are, and fortunately for us, he does not leave us like he found us. The degree of our response to his acceptance does not alter the fact that Jesus died for us: "While we were still sinners, Christ died for us" (Rom. 5:8). God does not accept us based on our qualifications. Neither should qualifications be the basis upon which we accept ourselves.

If forgiving is an action, what are you going to do now? You could go and tell the people who hurt you that you have forgiven them. In most cases, they will be glad to hear it but they probably will not really understand. (I found myself wanting to tell them I had forgiven them so they would know what they had done.)

When Vicki and I began the process of forgiveness,

we went to some of our new friends. We had told them about our church and they knew something about this kind of forgiveness. We declared our forgiveness to them person by person, incident by incident, as each came to mind. We told them we needed their help in maintaining our forgiveness. So, over the next few months, their gentle reminders helped us to stand firm in our decisions. To our great joy they found help from us in declaring and maintaining their forgiveness for those who had hurt them. Their hurt was not related to ours at all, but the remedy was the same. In the process, we recalled others outside the church whose sin had also hurt us and we forgave them too.

Forgiveness does not necessarily involve the restoration of a friendship with a former leader. Forgiveness restores our relationship to God. Only the true and total repentance of the leader can lead to mutual restoration.

We all have a tendency to take responsibility for the things others have done to us while avoiding responsibility for our own sin and the things we have done to others. Forgiveness deals with the things they did, and repentance deals with the things we did or did not do. Many of us know that in spite of what others did to us, there are mistakes we have made, as well as things we have done and things we have not done. Thus, we are doing the "penance of perpetual regret." We are experiencing an ongoing sense of loss, and are not able to do anything about it.

REPENTANCE

For Followers

What does the word repentance bring to mind? Is it only former leaders who must repent? Please do not confuse the apologies of some of our former leadership with repentance. Repentance goes beyond saying "I'm sorry," "I'm sorry *if* you were hurt," or even "I'm sorry you were hurt." This is not repentance, it is just remorse. Apologies are not repentance. Apologies are reactions to the consequences of my sin, not to the sin itself. Apologies can be an attempt at a payback for wrongs committed. Those who apologize rather than repent find it frustrating that those they have hurt will not just let the matter drop. They know God has forgiven them and cannot understand why others continue to feel bad about them after they have said they are sorry. A hardening of the heart develops.

By contrast, repentance leads to a softening of the heart. Repentance is humble recognition of a hunger in my heart for God. Repentance is my response to the horror of my sinfulness before God's holiness. Repentance comes when I recognize sin for what it is, call it what it is, and admit I am utterly helpless to make the correct changes by myself.

Biblical repentance involves confession and cleansing. First John 1:9 says, "If we confess our sins, he is faithful and just to forgive our sins and to cleanse us from all unrighteousness." He is faithful to forgive and just to cleanse. We confess; he cleanses. Our inadequate attempts to cleanse ourselves results in whitewash. Apologies without confession whitewash; confession cleanses. We are commanded to confess our sins, not sin. This means be specific, name names, give specific instances— as many as God reveals to you. Confession is specific.

The confession in 1 John 1:9 points back to verse 7, "But, if we walk in the light, as he is in the light, we have fellowship with one another and the blood of Jesus, his Son, purifies us from every sin." Confession is clearly in the context of fellowship. If we are going to be cleansed, we are going to have to bring what has been in the darkness into the light. This book may help you see what was in the darkness, but only you can bring it into the light.

Some of you were in situations where you were required to confess your sin, in confidence, in a small group. Later that confidence was betrayed by your leader. A means of access to God's grace had been stolen from you. But Jesus Christ is able to restore confession to a place of healing for you. You will find someone who can be trusted.

What are we repenting from? It does not have to do with our abuse or the fact that we went along with it. We have to repent from every one of those things that we did (and continue to do) that kept us from having to face God and ourselves on the basis of anything else but his grace alone. My calm exterior covered the icehouse that kept my soul in a deep freeze. No one could get near enough for me to feel them. Not even God. Not even after I decided to go to seminary.

Some we know have hidden in their anger, others behind tears of continuing sorrow determined to never allow themselves to be hurt again. What is keeping you living independently from God and from a real life? Does the idea of reckless abandon to the love of God disturb you? Does trusting God bring with it the feeling that you will probably be disappointed? Confess it. Allow God to cleanse you.[4]

For Leaders

Some former followers were also leaders. As leaders, you may feel the need to confess to those who once followed you. This is not the same as an apology. The objective is not to restore the relationship or seek their forgiveness. That is up to them. With confession you are removing a barrier between you and God.

You might begin by acknowledging that you have

abused him or her, sometimes consciously for your own gain or unconsciously because you were deceived by the teaching. Let God remind you of specific instances. Remember Millie, the young woman who worked in our home? I was completely deceived by the teaching, but pretending that my wife and I should not help her clean up was prideful selfishness.

You will want to accept complete responsibility. Do not blame those over you or their doctrines for what you did to your followers. Be prepared to consider your former follower's assessments of what you have done.[5]

You should avoid at all costs trying to pastor the former follower through his or her struggles, even if that is what they want. Acknowledge your own struggles and agree to mutual prayer. Do not allow yourself to enter relationships where you could abuse again.

Breaking the Yoke

In the name of accountability, our leaders exercised unholy control over all areas of our lives. We were manipulated into violating our consciences, into doing the will of man, and into believing it was the will of God. We looked to our pastors and our fellowship for spiritual provision that rightfully only comes from God. The degree to which we submitted our will to the will of another in order to find God's will is the extent of our involvement in "witchcraft."

We must realize who our enemy is. It is not Charles Simpson, Bob Mumford, Derek Prince, Don Basham, Ern Baxter, our husband, wife, father, or former pastor. The Enemy is the One who managed to obscure the Cross for us by tricking us to put our trust in men. The Enemy is the One who deceived us when we submitted to men in ways that we should only have submitted to God. Our enemy's name is Satan.

We must be very clear—our leaders did not practice witchcraft. But the continuous, subtle manipulation on certain aspects of our lives was just as sure a barrier in our walk with God. The kind of control over my life that I permitted, believing it was biblical, amounted to idolatry. I committed to a man what should only be committed to God, and expected to receive from a man what can only come from God. Thinking I was doing God's will, I was actually committing spiritual adultery. It has been a three-year process of facing it, renouncing it, and learning how to walk with God again.

Accountability is a word that then had to be redeemed for us. Accountability is not control. It is only a safety net. It does not determine what we will or will not do. We are the only ones who can ultimately know and do the will of God for our lives. Accountability keeps us from breaking our necks as we step out in faithfulness to God.

EFFECTS OF UNHOLY RELATIONSHIPS

On Adults

In interviews with those formerly involved in the shepherding movement, we found a fairly consistent inability for them to make real friends and to experience true fellowship with other believers. This confirmed our own experience. After leaving the movement, we were unable to be vulnerable. We often hear others say what we feel, "It is hard to trust people anymore, even those who want to be my friend," or, "I don't think that I can ever be vulnerable enough again to be a real friend," and the saddest of all, "I am never going to put myself in a place to be hurt by anybody again, it's just not worth the pain."

One couple we know is struggling with anger because they are unable to trust anyone to treat them honestly. When they were in the movement they appeared to have friends, and the husband even led a small group for a time. No one knew about their feelings of isolation that began as they tried to reach a standard of living that was unattainable for them. They found they had worked to reach a goal that did not have anything to do with what God wanted for them. In fact, they realized that very little that they had done "as unto the Lord" actually lifted him up. Rather, "as unto the Lord" was actually what their pastor thought was the best for them. Eventually they came face to face with the fact that they had traded obedience to the Lord for submission to a pastor.

Because questioning was a sign of disloyalty and a cause for mistrust, the very people to whom our friends had given their lives did not understand when this seemingly loyal couple began to question what was happening in their lives. They were no longer going to take the word of their pastor as being sufficient. Finally, our friend was left with self-doubt about his own ability to determine clearly what was best for him. He found he had problems believing that he could hear clearly from God without the help of anyone else.

We have another close friend who found herself in a situation where she had decided to participate in a certain group, but just was not happy with the outcome. The group was not what she had expected and she was uncomfortable with committing her time and energy to continue. Vicki asked why she did not just quit, and after looking at Vicki strangely for a minute, our friend smiled. Her next comment was, "Well, I guess I could, couldn't I?" The idea of quitting had never occurred to her before.

She said that she often feels paralyzed when trying to make a decision. For years her decisions had been made for her or offered as suggestions in such a way that the answer was obvious. Eventually she learned to feel that she could not make a good decision on her own. Now, she can't trust herself to make the right choices at all—she feels too vulnerable.

Forgiveness and repentance will deal with underlying issues, but there may also be some spiritual residue from a former relationship that is coloring our perspective without our knowing it. After confessing our reluctance to be vulnerable to God and others, Vicki and I had to renounce the remaining inability to be vulnerable as we would a curse, knowing that Jesus bore it for us and broke its power.

On Vows or Covenants

A related area of difficulty is vows or covenants made under false or distorted understandings. This is a delicate area since both the Old and New Testaments affirm that a vow before God should not be entered into lightly. But, in the Old Testament one who made a vow could not seek to be released from it, but a way was made for its redemption, usually by substitution. This was how the Old Covenant or Testament was redeemed by the New. Hebrews 9:15 says, "For this reason Christ is the mediator of a new covenant, that those who are called may receive the promised eternal inheritance—now that he has died as a ransom to set them free from the sins committed under the first covenant." God did not try to nullify the Old Covenant. He redeemed it with the New.

Covenants of unholy submission to a pastor or vows of unholy responsibility for fellow believers need to be confessed and redeemed by God's grace. Redemption involves the transference of our former misdirected submission from men to God. There is grace at the Cross for all our mistakes.

In the same way, vows of submission of a wife to a

husband may need to be reexamined. Our wedding vows were written by Charles Simpson and were used frequently throughout the shepherding churches. They bound Vicki to me in a kind of submission that should be reserved for God alone. In much the same way, our vows bound me to provide her those things that only God can provide. Vicki had to renounce me as her "savior and lord," and accept Christ as her only Savior and Lord. I also resigned as her "lord and savior" and accepted her as an "heir together of the graces of life." During the writing of this book, we redeemed our vows in a formal, public ceremony.

Many couples' marriages were "arranged" by their shepherds. Now that they are out of the church their marriage relationship has somehow lost its context. The command "What God has joined together, let no man separate" (Matt. 19:6), feels like a prison sentence to someone who knows it was man who joined them together. Only the Holy Spirit can assure you that whatever circumstances of unholy submission brought you together, God has joined you. You may also want to renew your vows.

Some women who have thus rejected the hierarchical model of marriage fear that they will be labeled "feminists." But many modern secular feminists simplistically equate male with cold, and masculine with oppressive. They reason that God (if there is one), must be feminine to be truly loving. Thus, Jesus was really a hermaphrodite—male in form, but female in character. But these are the conclusions of those who have essentially rejected God and his Word.[6] Secular feminists make interpretation mistakes that are very similar to the ones we made. They take principles out of context. They superimpose aspects of present culture onto the Scriptures making them appear to say things never intended by the original authors. One does not have to be a feminist to reject the

hierarchical understanding of marriage. No secular feminist can completely understand the Christian marriage of
mutual submission. It is not chauvinist or feminist; it's
miraculous!

On Children

Older children appear to suffer in essentially the
same manner as anyone under unholy authority. It is
helpful for them to make the same renunciation of father
as "savior and lord," and accept Christ just as a wife
should. Another helpful declaration for them to make is,
"God is not like my father." Our experience has shown
that hierarchical home situations can be somewhat intrin-
sically abusive in themselves, whether or not the parents
are sincere. The result for the child is a distorted image of
God. Natural teenage self-assertiveness can cover hurts
suffered while the family is in a shepherding church, but
when these hurts are later brought into a marriage, the
feelings can be overwhelming.

Several prominent Christian counselors regard, and
we believe rightly so, some of our practices of marital
submission and authority as spouse abuse.[7] As the Lord
leads, instances of manipulation and control that violated
the conscience or personhood of a child or wife, must be
confessed and renounced. The Holy Spirit will cleanse
and heal.

DEEPER NEEDS

In the shepherding movement, authority is the
answer to every need, and rebellion is the underlying
source of every problem. Every problem is relational and
every solution involves the application of more authority.
Remember Bobby Renn, Burt Reynolds' old friend? Until
recently, I believed that if we had been able to teach him

about submission, the application of godly authority would have saved his life. There are plenty of people whose lives turned around dramatically when they submitted themselves and their problems to a pastor. But in most cases, conformity to external authority only masks whatever deeper conflicts we brought into the movement. When authority is removed these problems tend to bubble up to the surface again. Alcoholism, the consequences of child sexual abuse, spouse abuse, and whole areas of problems that have been submerged in submission resurface to threaten our marriages, our sanity, and our trust in God's love.

We have found that the resources of the greater body of Christ have vastly increased in recent years. A whole new discipline of professional pastoral counseling has arisen to address these problems in Christians. You do not have to go through it alone.

A WORD OF CAUTION

Eventually, we who have been abused by the shepherding movement will find our way into some kind of fellowship. In our experience, fellowship has been crucial to our recovery so far. The goal now is to avoid falling into the same kinds of traps. How can we learn to give ourselves again without getting burned? How can we tell if a particular group is going to become abusive? There are many groups promising that they have examined the problems of the shepherding movement and have kept the best while eliminating the worst. They offer former followers intense commitment, fellowship, and worship—without abuse..

We do not wish to condemn the beliefs or practices of any group. We know how we got into trouble and how we have avoided re-abuse. We suggest a simple observation, and we offer the following for the benefit of those who wish to avoid what has happened to us. Examine any church or group for signs of an understanding that spiritual leadership involves a chain of command.

Any church has within it a "Christian organization" that must function in the world. This part of the church may involve a military model of organization. A leader may require a volunteer or paid assistant to type and mail a letter today and expect it will happen just because he or she said so. This is not the same as spiritual authority. The leader has a job to do and the assistant has volunteered or is being paid to help get that job done. The focus is mutual concern for the job, not the relationship.

If the idea of a spiritual chain of command does not appear to be present in the church, look at the position of women. Is there a hierarchy of roles in the home? Is submission mutual or one way? No matter what is said of leadership in the church, if they buy into the home as a hierarchy, logically they must in some way see the workings of the church as a spiritual hierarchy. That church may be doing great things and its members may be producing good fruit, but it is not for us.

LOVING AGAIN

There are two sure ways many of us are avoiding further hurt. One is by staying out of any form of church or Christian fellowship altogether. The other is to attend a church so large that we will never get close to anyone and no one will ever ask us to do anything. While we have found both actions to be important parts of the process, they do not actually bring healing. Getting on with our lives in Christ means having fellowship and being vulnerable to it in some way.

Ultimate redemption for unholy relationships is the formation of true Christian friendships. Jesus' command is not to relate to one another, but to love one another.

We have found it both very difficult and very rewarding to be vulnerable to new friends. The fellowship of true friends provides the context for God's love to heal us.

Real friendships provide us with opportunities to testify to each new nuance of God's work in our lives. Like forgiveness and confession, testimony to friends brings the work of God into the light. Revelation 12:11 refers to an "accuser" who wants to keep us from being healed.

> They overcame him
> by the blood of the Lamb
> and by the word of their testimony;
> they did not love their lives so much
> as to shrink from death.

We overcome because of the Cross—the "blood of the Lamb"—and by our testimony of God's grace. Testimony exposes our lives to others. It is risky, but, if we love our lives too much to testify, our gains will keep slipping away. "The man who loves his life will lose it" (John 12:25).

THE WAY BACK

Vicki and I have walked through each of these areas on our way out. We have found the way out to also be the way back—back to where we were first "called." We have met former followers who initially chose discipleship as their means of preparation for some form of full-time vocational Christian ministry. We did not have a specific sense of calling to preach in a specific denomination or to go to a specific mission field, but when I was eighteen or nineteen, I sensed that "the ministry" was going to be my career. Vicki had the same general feeling.

The shepherding movement left us with a kind of paralysis toward "the work of the Lord." There never seemed to be a place of usefulness for us. Eventually we adopted the mind-set that there was nothing for us to do. Besides, whatever we were able to do, there was always someone who could do it so much better.

We now understand that God has called each one of us, not because he needs our talents, but just because each one of us is unique. He has voluntarily limited himself in such a way that he cannot minister to some of those in need in exactly the way he wants through someone else. He wants you. Someone out there needs exactly what God has given you. Yes, he can find someone else, but it just wouldn't be the same without you.

AFTER THE LOCUSTS

We heard an altar call at a church we visited that expressed the pressing need to become a Christian and enter into God's service: "For all sad words of tongue or pen, The saddest are these: 'It might have been!' "[8] The promise made to Israel in Joel 2:25–26 has been a source of hope for us when we wonder about what might have been:

> I will repay you for the years
> the locusts have eaten. . .
> You will have plenty to eat, until you are full,
> and you will praise the name of the LORD your God,
> who has worked wonders for you;
> never again will my people be shamed.'

What have the "locusts" eaten in your life? How many years have they been feasting? For fifteen years, we waited for the system to approve us for ministry so that we could get on with God's call. In one year, while attending seminary, we prayed and counseled with over one hundred people and have seen God work wonders. One friend remarked, "You realize that is more counseling than the average parish minister gets to do in a lifetime!" God has indeed repaid us for "the years the locusts have eaten!"

As Vicki and I have returned to our call to extend the mercy of God to his church and the world, we have found that sharing whatever we can to encourage the hurting is part of our own recovery. As you do business with God don't be surprised if you experience, as we have, the next verses of Joel's prophecy:

And afterward,
I will pour out my Spirit on all people.
Your sons and daughters will prophesy,
   your old men will dream dreams,
   your young men will see visions.
Even on my servants, both men and women,
   I will pour out my Spirit in those days. . .
And everyone who calls
   on the name of the LORD will be saved;
for on Mount Zion and in Jerusalem
   there will be deliverance. . .
among the survivors. . .

Joel 2:28–29, 32

There will be "deliverance. . .among the survivors." There is within you a measure of the presence of the Holy Spirit that is only known through suffering. You will find as he restores you, others will be freed by God's grace because of you and your testimony. Get back to being filled with Jesus' love and letting it spill out on everyone else.

When first sent forth to minister the word,
Say did we preach ourselves or Christ the Lord?
Was it our aim disciples to collect,
To raise a party or to found a sect?
No; but to spread the power of Jesus' name,
Repair the walls of our Jerusalem
Revive the piety of ancient days,
And fill the earth with our redeemer's praise.

—Charles Wesley

VICKI'S EPILOGUE

Several times since Ron and I started this project, I have heard myself say: "This is too hard, let's quit!" "It is not worth all this pain, I don't want to talk about it anymore!" And the biggie, "I can't believe we are going to tell everyone how stupid we were!"

Now, as we finish the final rewrite, I find myself with various feelings about the whole experience. To say that this was difficult would be an understatement. So much has changed for us during the fourteen months of seeing this book to completion. We have put the last fifteen years of our lives under a microscope. It is one thing to share your life with friends and counselors but quite another to put it into print. But through it all, we have learned that God is eternally faithful to his children and he has been to us.

I regret that some of our friends will not be pleased that we have told our story. I know that those who embrace the Cross will be in for a painful process of facing their years and the long walk to healing. My own walk out is not complete either. But the joy I do know now is that I am walking toward Jesus. I am gaining a sense of who I am in Christ and the sense that my place with him is as important as anyone else's.

NOTES

INTRODUCTION

[1]Robert Digitale, "An Idea Whose Time Has Gone?" *Christianity Today* 34, no. 5 (March 1990): 38.

[2]Ibid., 40.

[3]Ibid., 40.

[4]Randy Frame, "Maranatha Disbands as Federation of Churches," *Christianity Today* 34, no. 5 (March 1990): 41.

[5]Flavil Yeakley, *The Discipling Dilemma* (Nashville: Gospel Advocate, 1988), 84.

[6]Ibid., 206.

CHAPTER 1

[1]Michael Harper, *Three Sisters* (Wheaton: Tyndale, 1979), 92.

[2]Ibid., 94.

CHAPTER 2

[1]Michael Harper, *Three Sisters* (Wheaton: Tyndale, 1979), 94.

CHAPTER 6

[1]The story is related in Charles Simpson's *The Challenge to Care* (Ann Arbor: Servant, 1986), 21.

[2]For the means of expression of our feelings in the last two sentences, we are indebted to Dan B. Allender, *The Wounded Heart* (Colorado Springs: NavPress, 1990), 78.

CHAPTER 7

[1]We are again indebted to Dan Allender and page 78 of *The Wounded Heart* for the ideas that express our feelings in the last two sentences.

[2]Michael Harper, *Three Sisters* (Wheaton: Tyndale, 1979). See page 141. He cites the 1975 "Ann Arbor Report," a "theological and pastoral evaluation of the current controversy over 'discipleship' and 'shepherding.' "

[3]_____, Appendix C.

[4]Ronald M. Enroth, "The Power Abusers," *Eternity*, October 1979, 25.

[5]Bob Mumford, in the column "New Wine Forum," *New Wine Magazine*, June 1974, 30.

[6]Charles Simpson, "Making Disciples," *New Wine Magazine*, March 1974, 6.

[7]Ern Baxter, "Becoming a Love Slave," *New Wine Magazine*, October 1975.

[8]Charles Simpson, "The Salt of the Covenant, Loyalty," *New Wine Magazine*, December 1975.

[9]_____, "Faithful in Natural Things," *New Wine Magazine*, September 1975, 24.

[10]Ibid., 25.

[11]Ibid., 25.

[12]Ibid., 26.

[13]Ibid., 29.

[14]Glen Roachelle, "Distinguishing the Extraordinary From the Ordinary," *New Wine Magazine*, February 1986, 22.

CHAPTER 8

[1]Bob Mumford, "Fatherpower," *New Wine Magazine*, April 1978, 6.

[2]David and Vera Mace, *We Can Have Better Marriages* (Nashville: Abingdon, 1974), 39.

[3]We gratefully present in edited form, sections of Dr. Fred Layman's, "Male Headship in Paul's Thought," *Wesleyan Theological Journal* 1 (Spring 1980): 49. He has helped us retain the basic thrust of his article.

[4]Ibid., 55.

[5]Ibid.

[6]Ibid., 52.

[7]Ibid., 54.

CHAPTER 9

[1]Kenneth Willis Clark, "The Meaning of [*Kata*] *Kyrieyein*," in *Studies in New Testament Language and Text*, ed.J. K. Elliot (Leiden: Brill, 1976), 100–105.

[2]Stephen Charles Mott, *Biblical Ethics and Social Change* (New York: Oxford University Press, 1982), 195.

[3]Charles Simpson, "Joints, God's Divine Network of Supply to the Body of Christ," *New Wine Magazine*, February 1976, 8.

[4]Ibid.

[5]"New Wine Forum, Discipleship," *New Wine Magazine*, March 1974, 30.

[6]Charles Simpson, "Making Disciples," *New Wine Magazine*, March 1974, 9.

[7]Ibid.

[8]Charles Simpson, *The Challenge to Care* (Ann Arbor: Servant, 1986), 164.

[9]Bert Gehezzi, "Bob Mumford, after Discipleship," *Charisma and Christian Life*, August 1987, 26.

[10]Ibid., 27.

[11]Charles Simpson, "A Special Announcement," *New Wine Magazine*, October 1985, 46–47.

[12]Charles Simpson, "Working with God," *New Wine Magazine*, September 1985, 10.

CHAPTER 10

[1]Henri Nouwen, *Making All Things New* (New York: Harper & Row, 1981).

[2]We gratefully acknowledge that the basic outline for this teaching on the Cross was suggested by a message given by Derek Prince, November, 1989.

[3]Suggested by ideas in Allender, *The Wounded Heart* (Colorado Springs: NavPress, 1990), 200.

[4]Ibid., 204–6.

[5]Ibid., 236.

[6]Suggested by material from Donald M. and Robbie B. Joy, *Lovers, Whatever Happened to Eden?* (Waco: Word 1987), 44-45.

[7]James Alsdurf and Phyllis Alsdurf, *Battered Into Submission* (Downers Grove: InterVarsity, 1989), 81.

[8]John Greenleaf Whittier, *Maud Muller*, stanza 53.